Nobel Neocolonialism: U.S. West Asian, North and East African Foreign Policy Under the Obama Administration

TORRANCE
STEPHENS

Other books by Torrance Stephens

a matter of attention - novel
fast and gamin' – short stories
butter brown – short stories
rockstar, stud, gigolo – short stories
late nite winds of club paradise – poetry
anonymous guest – poetry
for u who left me while I slept - poetry
brilliant dumb – essays
dirt behind my ears – essays
negro comfortable – essays
discourses and views on the african american experience
in the early twenty-first century - essays

RAW DOG BUFFALO PRESS
PALMETTO/MEMPHIS/WHEREVER
© 2016 BY
TORRANCE STEPHENS
@RAWDAWGBUFFALO

"Colonialism hardly ever exploits the whole of a country. It contents itself with bringing to light the natural resources, which it extracts, and exports to meet the needs of the mother country's industries, thereby allowing certain sectors of the colony to become relatively rich. But the rest of the colony follows its path of underdevelopment and poverty, or at all events sinks into it more deeply."

Frantz Fanon from The Wretched of the Earth

I won't be a party to a conspiracy to mobilize the Arabs against the Persians. Only the forces of **colonialism** benefit from such a conspiracy. I won't be a party to a conspiracy that splits Islam into two - Shiite Islam and Sunni Islam – mobilizing Sunni Islam against Shiite Islam.

Muammar Gaddafi

"The mistakes of the Iraq war are not only tactical and strategic, but historical. It is essentially a war of **colonialism**, attempted in the post-colonial age."

Zbigniew Brzezinski

Nobel Neocolonialism: U.S. West Asian, North and East African Foreign Policy Under the Obama Administration

TORRANCE
STEPHENS

1

Something caught my eye while reading my favorite Russian News daily - the Kommersant. Kyrgyzstan, which is located in Asia in between Kazakhstan, Tajikistan and China, just kicked out the only representative of the United States military in the region. Manas Air Force Base, which may be our closest military base to Russia, will be no longer in about 6 months. The base is only about 8 or 9 years old and was formed ex post facto to 911. Not that this is an indication of how the new administration's relationship with Russia will be in the future (which it is) or the fact that Russia is flexing, and will continue to be a thorn in the side of America's foreign policy objectives (which it is), but more so how this will play with respect to the administrations locution concerning Afghanistan. Manas is most likely our major supply hub to troops in Afghanistan. The President of this small nation, Kurmanbek Bakiyev made his announcement ironically right after the Russian government agreed to give his country $2.1 billion in economic aid.

As we read, tweet, blog and type the war in Afghanistan is growing and becoming more out of control each day. President Obama stated last week that an additional 17,000 troops are on their way to Afghanistan. This is strange to me when the current president of the country, Hamid Karzai, was not involved in the decision to add more troops into his country? However, he was "informed of the deployments via a telephone call from Obama" on February 17.

I do not know what to anticipate with respect to the new administration's approach to Afghanistan. I do hope that they do more than just chase the Taliban around the country back and forth; to and from Pakistan. Meaning he cannot continue the Bush approach, for Bush was so busy palling up with the former military dictator/president of Pakistan that he dropped the ball on Russia. And as of now, it seems as if Obama has been so enthralled, that he has over looked Russia for the player they are on the world stage, especially in their own backyard

A while back I wrote that Obama needed do some serious consideration with regard to his dealings with Russia, specifically that Russia "may be the first head bump for him… Russia (Putin) is making a fat cat move to buy allegiance from Latin American states that are right in our backyard. Plus they're upset with our decision to deploy elements of a missile defense system in Poland and the Czech Republic. As a result, they have decided to place some similar equipment in Cuba – or so they say. That was then, now he's cock blocking with respect to U.S. war efforts in Afghanistan. I can't wait for this will make for some good opinion editorials for me to write on.

2

If you ask the average African American about China, they will probably say very little with the exception of the query, why do they own the neighborhood soul food restaurant. If you asked what impact does U.S.-China relations have on them, you may draw a quixotic stare, as I did recently.

This week China's President Hu Jin Tao was in the United States for the first time since 2006 to meet with President Barack Obama. The goal, I suspect, based on the needs of the United States, the Economic tension with China, and other concerns is to both reframe and redefine the relationship between the U.S. and China. So far so good, already Obama has encouraged the President to acknowledge that China has a long way to go with respect to human rights as well as secured $45 billion in investments from the nation. Add to that, the announcement affirming energy deals that will engender partnerships with U.S. and Chinese energy companies to develop clean energy.

What is of importance for me is to discern how these efforts will impact the African American community and what it means for us? What I can surmise thus far is that if we are to benefit equally from interaction between these two nations, we must get our stuff in order. First, it means that we will have to become financially literate. Most of us do not know anything about the Yuan, let alone exchange rates and currency market periods as it relates to the dollars in our pocket or our personal economic bottom line.

It also asserts that we need to become innovative as a community to take advantage of any opportunities that may engender due to stronger U.S.-China economic interaction. This mean making our children learn Mandarin, study harder, and focus on the sciences and math as opposed to sports or music. Otherwise we will not be in a position to take advantage of the skills required to go after the marginal dollars available in these areas around the world.

Looking at it logistically, the only other option for us will be to join the military, for unlike China, that's where a large corpus of U.S. spending is directed. The Chinese spend billions around the world on natural resources to expand and sustain their manufacturing base while we spend the same amount on funding two wars in Iraq and Afghanistan.

Education and immigration issues will be of major importance for the Obama administration and African Americans need to push for changes that will enhance both. Mathematically, we need to be able to sell goods, services, and skills if we are to move forward on an equal economic footing. We are a nation of 300 million compared to 1.3 billion in china – we need to be involved in this market. Thus, the importance of education specifically for African Americans and all Americans for that matter cannot be overlooked. The deal with energy companies mentioned earlier mainly deals with developing carbon capturing technologies and clean coal technology, and frankly, we will miss the boat if we do not engage in these areas and understand what is at stake for us.

Plain and simple, many of us write off the importance of understanding the China-U.S. relationship yet wonder why we maintain the same economic status as a community decade after decade. If we truly desire to reap the benefits of an African American president, then we need to study policy and make it work for us and stop kvetching about things that are not really that important.

3

I heard it mentioned during his state of the union address, how Obama alluded to Tunisia and Egypt in a backhanded way - saying we support democracy everywhere people call for such. This is safe and as some would say "all good", but do we really? Is it just rhetoric promulgated in the kvetching of votes for an upcoming election?

I can't answer that, but it is my perception that America does not support democracy and what we see occurring in the Arab world places new definition to the biblical statement of "a measure of wheat for a penny" and how this single sentiment in addition to the U.S. position in the region can topple a government. Sure, we saw turmoil in Turkey, Ireland, Brittan, and France but these homogenous democratic governments saw disruption based on falling economic systems. In North Africa and the Arab world what we are observing is a function of food and despotism, totalitarian rule and the simple desire to provide for one's family, and to live as a free thinking individual. This is completely different from what we observed in Europe.

In fact it could be argued that we, America, created this monster and it may reflect badly about how we go about democracy building around the world. We take the approach of overthrowing an established government and then installing our own and call it nation building. The problem is that true nation building can only occur from the citizenry. We have created a monster, all these years, we have stood by and support tyrants who never supported democratic rule for our own purpose of a so-called peace with Israel or our war on the emotion we call terror.

Zine el Abidine Ben Ali had ruled for 23 years before he had to flee Tunisia. Hosni Mubarak has ruled Egypt for three decades. Hypothetically, if a take-over occurs, it will prevent Mubarak from handing power down to his son. I figure the U.S. believes the hype regarding the Ikhwan (Muslim Brotherhood) that they will possibly fill the leadership void. After all, we all know Hamas is the Palestinian wing of the Muslim brotherhood.

Again, we have created this problem and the unfortunate thing is that Obama via consequences will have to deal with new threats to stabilization in the region. If Egypt falls then there will be no peace in Israel. More dangerous is what will happen if Yemen falls. In Sana, at least 10,000 protesters gathered at Sana University and thousands more in other parts of the small Arab nation and more gathered elsewhere, participants, lawmakers, and activists reached by telephone said. Many carried pink banners and wore pink headbands. The situation in Yemen is a lot more dangerous than in any other Arab country. If it becomes unstable, being the new foundation for al Qaeda, it may become another Somalia. And just yesterday, we saw massive protest in Amman, Jordan.

All in all American politics is seeing the outcome of its misdirected approach to foreign policy and it is a shame that it has to manifest during the watch of Obama. For years U.S. foreign policy in the Middle East and Arabian Peninsula has pushed, unwittingly, in our special rakish way, for what we say

6

we do not desire – Arab radicalization. And we did this by ignoring our own values and democratic principles. We ignored the Palestinian problem, supported for years unconditionally the oppression of citizens by autocratic rulers via our interest in a war on terror, and an artificial peace for Israel. Now we have what we created: folks that hate us even more since all these places are run for now by Western supported leaders.

4

As the Egyptian people take to the streets of its cities against decades of repression, increasing poverty, and unbearable food prices, the Obama administration is in an admitted quandary of either supporting the requested demand for democratic reform of the people or the stable support of a corrupt dictator. The longer he waits to decide in pursuit of his request for an "orderly transition" to democratic reform as stated by Secretary of State Hillary Clinton, the more his hopes of modeling changes as those that occurred in Turkey, the more likely what happened in Iran in 1979 will come to fruition. The conundrum is that he as president in the past has been in bed with Mubarak and King Abdullah of Saudi Arabia too long to adapt or alter American political policy in the region. This in fact is worse than the BP oil spill or the mid-term election losses the democrats suffered this past November.

The citizenry of Egypt know more of the U.S. support of Mubarak's three decades than the average American and of the $1.5 billion annually it gives to his totalitarian regime. This is an overshadowing sticking point since cutting off this aid would likely make the Israeli government uneasy. Being on the wrong side of history could proffer even more hazards for President Obama: for again it may result in leadership similar to that in Iran after the overthrow of the shah via popular revolt – but I seriously doubt it.

Yet it could. We have already lost face validity for even asking a man who has ruled for nearly 30 years to be in charge of the democratic conversion of an autocratic state. I would be more fearful of an anti-American state more so than an Islamic fundamentalist state that hates the West. I remember seeing the murder of Anwar Sadat on television and remember that it was not by Islamic fundamentalist but rather people who hated the fact that he dealt with the West, particularly the United States and Israel. I also recall that our most hated enemy, Al Zawahiri, was forced to leave his home of Egypt because of Mubarak's preventing such men from being a part of the political process. Thus it is not unlikely that these young secular democracy seeking, Twitter, and Facebook users may be pushed by Obama's inaction to hate the U.S. as much or as equal as Mubarak.

Obama seems to need to brush up on his history or risk another Khomeini. The truth is we back step when people desire liberty and democracy after we talk it up as did the president in his address at the American University in Cairo in 2009. We go after the Saddam Hussein's of the world while kicking it with the Mubarak's and King Abdullah's of the world. This is what creates Islamic fundamental extremist that desire to fly planes into our architecture. We have learned nothing after supporting Augusto Pinochet in Chile, Chiang Kaishek in Tiawan or Mobutu Seko in Zaire. Obama needs to face the fact that we support such openly, especially in the case of Mubarak. The sad thing is that we support Israel, who just sent three Israeli planes landed at Cairo's Mina International Airport on Saturday carrying hazardous equipment for use in dispersing and suppressing large crowds. It is as if we seem to speak more of the Suez canal and what Egypt thinks and fees than of the people of Egypt.

Obama has a tough task ahead. He holds the baggage of American foreign policy. This will make it complicated for him to urge a transition from a U.S. supported government that has abrogated any and all other organized political alternatives and elides political freedom. Maybe we should rethink Afghanistan for what we see in Tunisia and Egypt tells us that it does not require a bloody, bellicose, and illegal invasion and occupation to overthrow a dictator. So get your practice on Mr. President, Jordan is likely to be next - so don't blow it.

5

The events of the past weeks have served as a dramatic wake up call for President Obama and his retinue of advisors, as well as America as a whole regarding rc-thinking their approaches to foreign policy in North Africa, the Middle east, and worldwide. Although most African Americans are familiar with Egypt and the turmoil occurring across its chronicled cities and other nation states in the region, grievously most have a curbed comprehension of the impact these occurrences have on President Obama and any policy deliberated as a function of these events. The conundrum from this vantage point for President Obama and his administration is not purely formulating policy for America, but conspicuously deciding how to formulate policy on behalf of Israel and other ally's in the region or the inchoate masses of the secular populations in revolt.

First and foremost is addressing emotion, better known as terror, as a singular attribute that Americans alone confront in concert with dealing with autocrats all for the good of us, under the guise of peace and Islamic fundamentalism. Mistakes made some 30 years ago in Iran, and what we have observed in Egypt and Libya, still fall on deaf ears – even for the prophet of all prophets Obama. In addition, our monolithic approach to supporting what is best for Israel and a myopic focus on Al Qaeda is misplaced and may do more harm than good. Common sense would advocate looking at all nations singularly but our focus on terrorism prevents such. There are differences between military dictators and monarchs, but starvation, repression, discrimination, and poverty are least common dominators if one accepts and places the people of nations first.

In Libya, The United States is openly spoken out against the violence in the country's second-largest city, Benghazi, where there are reports of security forces firing on peaceful protesters and where human-rights groups say many have been killed in recent days. In Iran, unconfirmed reports of anti-government gatherings on being broken up by a security police and members of the feared pro-government Basij militia patrolling the streets again he has spoken out.

The hand he is dealing with is progressively getting difficult to contain. There is Raymond Davis, the American who shot two men dead in Lahore, triggering a diplomatic crisis between Pakistan and the U.S. A former CIA agent, he opened fire with a semi-automatic Glock pistol on the two men who had pulled up in front of his car at a red light on 25 January. The 36-year-old former Special Forces soldier fired 10 shots and got out of his car to shoot one man twice in the back as he fled. A third man was crushed by an American vehicle as it rushed to Davis's aid. Police confiscated from his car: an unlicensed pistol, a long-range radio, a GPS device, an infrared torch, and a camera with pictures of buildings around Lahore. The possibility of unrest growing and spreading in the region and its impact on the price of oil and the recovering U.S. economy makes all of this even more difficult. We have already seen militant actions lead to blowing up Iraq's largest oil refinery.

This is the position Obama is in. His taciturn inactivity places us in more danger by ignoring this because the people for whom this really matters will not forget either his inactivity or ineptness when orating support for the likes of King Abdullah of Saudi Arabia, a Mubarak of Egypt, Bashar Assad of Syria, or King Hamad bin isa al-Khalife of Bahrain. President Obama needs to make a decision regarding what is next for Libya and the Middle East. He must not make the mistake of the past and he must be able to see that the protest in North Africa and the Arab world are closer to the protest observed here in America during the 60s and the civil rights era. Those movements are fueled by the youth of these nations just like it was the youth in the United States that hit the streets then. It will be difficult. On the one hand he will need to defend individual policy parameters that support nation building, and democracy and human rights; not just in North Africa and the Middle East, but Russia and China also. Additionally, he must re-establish U.S. credibility and form new relationships with the new leadership of Egypt, Tunisia, and other places if such comes to fruition; if not, engage the opposition leadership while maintaining close ties with the military of said countries.

This will mean changing the U.S. foreign policy assumption of a one size fits all approach. Outside of the region we may be able to learn a thing or two from the riots in Greece and India, and use this to re-evaluate what we did wrong for example in Iran in 1979. Regardless, this is a difficult situation he faces since it is obvious he has noted difficulty is siding with the ideas of freedom, liberty, and democracy for the citizenry or maintaining an autocratic association with a dictator for the sake of a quasi-peace for Israel, and good standing of the U.S. in the eyes of the region's other despots.

The president's talk has been top shelf, demanding change now, but it is rhetorical seeing that he and his state department are torn between advancing democracy in the region and the old school, approach that change "takes time. He should take into consideration that polity should be based on security and the well-being of the U.S. first and foremost.

Things in the Arab world will continue to surprise and if Obama is to maintain any type of control, he must become a student of history and learn from the mistakes of past U.S.

foreign policy. He has one advantage: he was opposite Rush Limbaugh, Glenn beck, Newt Gingrich, and Mike Huckabee who criticized the president for not Support Mubarak.

6

I find it surprising that almost three weeks after turmoil erupted in Libya, there is still no assertive policy position enumerated by the Obama administration. I know it is not easy to slap words on paper or read them from a teleprompter that will actually have weight and action. I do doubt the balls of all in Washington to address this conundrum inclusive of chairman of the Senate Foreign Relations Committee Jjohn Kerry and Senators John McCain and Joe Lieberman.

The President talks a mean game regarding "a range of potential options, including potential military options" but what is not stated is the problems of dealing with Libya while a future eruption in Saudi Arabia is likely eminent.

Like most other monarchs in the region, King Abdullah of Saudi Arabia may follow the Libyan colonel even though he has been offered economic bribes. Saudi Arabia recently mobilized 10,000 security personnel into its northeastern Shia Muslim provinces, according to reports, preparing for next week's "day of rage". This could be both a nightmare and headache for Saudi Arabia's Monarch and the Obama Administration who, it has been reported, are in talks with the Saudi's to get supplies and weapons to the Libyan opposition.

This new Arab awakening of rebellion in Saudi, namely from the Shia majority, is similar to what the administration is ignoring in the Sunni-dominated nation of Bahrain, where protesters are calling for the overthrow of the ruling al-Khalifa family. Obama knows that King Abdullah of Saudi Arabia is reported to have told the Bahraini that if they do not end the Shia revolt, he will.

At least 20,000 Saudis are expected to gather in Riyadh and in the Shia Muslim provinces of the north-east of the country in six days, in an effort to overthrow the House of Saud. In a desperate effort to avoid any outside news of the extent of the protests spreading the Saudi's have enacted fascist blogging regulations that prohibit non-citizens from writing about news and chat room users are being made to register with the government. Bloggers even need to obtain government licenses and to strictly abide by Islamic sharia law. "Internet sites containing video and audio materials" created from mobile phone/smartphone content will fall under the newspaper and be defined as falling under the Saudi Press and Publications Law.

Obama's problems are multiple. First, regarding Libya is the overall perception of America interfering in Middle Eastern and North African affairs as they did in Iraq and Kuwait while recanting the problems of being inactive as well as repeating what happened in Iraqi Kurdistan, Rwanda, and Bosnia and Herzegovina by not getting involved. Also, if the Saudi royal family, a "key ally" of the U.S. and one of the world's principal oil producers decides to use violence against demonstrators all hell will hit the fan, especially with oil prices near $120 a barrel.

I admit it is easy for me to sit on the side lines and ruminate on what I see and think based on my understanding of behavior and history. Sorry to say Obama and most politicians who are not blinded by singular lobbied issues cannot do the same. I guess there are no balls in Washington anymore.

7

President Obama is quick to join the protest against Republicans both inside and outside the Beltway. Likewise, his "on the job training" in dealing with social unrest in North Africa and the Arabian Peninsula is also prominent, especially when it makes him look grand standing on the side of democracy in Tunisia and Egypt. This is in stark contrast to the manner in which he deals with similar issues in Sub Saharan Africa.

There are several troubled spots in Sub Saharan Africa currently that neither the media, President Obama or his State department have addressed publically, most prominently are what is occurring in Uganda, The Ivory Coast, the Sudan or even what is occurring in Zimbabwe. In fact until today Obama has basically been quiet on what is occurring in the Ivory Coast.

In Uganda, President Museveni, the formal rebel leader has been in power ever since he took control of the nation twenty five years ago. He is a very close ally of the United States and receives 100's of millions of dollars in aid annually

– while the population is gripped in extreme poverty and joblessness. Obama has never addressed or spoken about the dozens of deaths that have been occurring since the 2009 youth protest against the government. Even this week, thousands took to the streets of Kampala but they are ignored and portrayed as invisible by the present U.S. administration.

In the Ivory Coast, after free and fair elections, Laurent Gbagbo still refuses to step down after losing the presidential elections this past November. Although this past December, President Barack Obama urged Ivory Coast's incumbent leader to cede power to the "legitimate winner" of the polls, he was not as forceful as he has been with his counterparts in North Africa or even in Iran. The United States has agreed with Ecowas that sanctions should be put in place but outside of that has shown no leadership on the issue. Meanwhile, Ivory Coast's incumbent leader has seized four major international banks that had shut down operations because the banks did not respect the law and closed without proper notice. The banks included offices for Britain's Standard Chartered, France's BNP–Paribas and Societe Generale along with U.S. bank Citibank.

In the Sudan, students, mobilized by online social networks, rioted in Khartoum, throwing stones at police cars and chanting. Unlike the recent uprising in Tunisia and the ongoing one in Egypt, but there is also the issue of southern Sudan's recent referendum vote, which approved secession from the north. As Khartoum is located in northern Sudan, it remains unclear what relation, if any, the uprising has to the recent referendum. One thing is clear, however: the winds of change are blowing across Africa and the Middle East, and whether they will bring stability and democracy or more civil war and dictatorship remains to be seen.

Prior to Tunisia's popular revolt, Sudan was the last Arab country to overthrow a leader with popular protests, ousting Jaafar Nimeiri in 1985. Just like the other recent revolts, the Sudan is in an economic crisis associated with government overspending and bloated import bills caused by foreign currency shortages and which have forced an effective devaluation of the Sudanese pound last year.

8

Deception as a tactic has both advantages and pitfalls. It seems that the Obama administration has not calculated nor considered either from their promotion, support, and initiation of a no fly zone over Libya. The overzealous mandate for the incessant bombs over the North African country makes me consider several issues that the main stream media and associated pundits have yet to consider let alone discuss.

First, the U.S. has no strategic or security interest in Libya or in seeing Gaddifi removed from power. Although the premise of protecting civilians is promulgated as being of utmost importance, they fail to promise to protect pro-government civilians if rebels start killing ruthlessly once they reach the immediate areas around Tripoli. This throws a wrench in what is apparently illogic U.S. logic.

Second, the hypocrisy displayed by the current administration causes additional consternation. Looking at Yemen for example, where in theory, we have a strategic interest, we are taking no action. Yemen is a country in which we have evidence that Al Qaeda is holding training for terrorist attacks against the U.S. There is also a division between the military defectors from the monarchy and those loyal to the U.S. confederate President Ali Abdullah Saleh. We are not involved at all yet a split in the military is likely the U.S.'s worse fear seeing that it may lead to isolation for our failure to openly and aggressively support the youth revolt. Already there are more anti-U.S. than most other Arab nations and this may push them closer to Al Qaeda.

This week in the small nation, rival tanks deployed in the streets after three senior army commanders defected to support protesters calling for the U.S.-backed president to step down. Last Friday President Saleh's forces opened fire from rooftops, killing more than 40 protestors. The United States, unlike its example in Libya of stating they need to protect the citizens – ignored this act completely.

We say that such a vacuum in Yemen may result in an opening for Al Qaeda politically. The same is true for Bahrain, Libya, and Saudi Arabia just to name a few but we only militarily get involved with Libya. Plus we see what our military excursion in Afghanistan has produced – no progress and a more enduring Taliban. We should have also been able to see what Iraq taught us – that billions of dollars and hundreds of thousands of troops cannot mandate democracy.

The United States and the West forget their historic colonial and imperialistic past when dealing with these nations and the fact that many of these places we call nations were never nations until others outside of the region drew the present day maps. Iraq is a region of Kurds, Sunni's and Shiite's we forced together. Afghanistan is a similar nomadic land, and many are run by autocrats in the form of monarchs.

This is our problem. Yes, the real reason we are using military might in Libya is because we want to take attention away for not being consistent in Bahrain, Yemen and Saudi Arabia. Places were kings and Sunni minorities rule oppressed Shiite majorities. Places where the use of force and guns on protestors cause more instability when we claim our worry is instability. The president was even protested in Brazil this week on his Latin American visit, and what did they use to break this protest: rubber bullets.

Our assault on Libya is misplaced and more like the move of a bully or a punk. Punks never deal with the problem at hand but rather they find a scapegoat to take attention away from the problem; which in this case is America's foreign policy and national security; which is not a function of Libya or Col. Muammar Quaddafi, but what happens in Yemen, Saudi Arabia and Bahrain is. We must never forget the lyrics of that classic hip hop song - "punks jump up to get beat down".

9

Not so long ago I remember comparing then President George W. Bush's entry into Afghanistan as being another Vietnam. It had no direction and unfortunately under the current administration, although it has instruction, it still is going every which way but loose. I remember Vietnam, seeing news every day of mangled bodies of young American soldiers barely out of high school fighting in mangrove swamps and being carried out mortally wounded on large helicopters, just as I remember the day we watched the draft and saw the birthday of my uncle, October 28, the only male in my family, listed on the draft board on television. He was lucky, being the only male he was not taken in the draft.

The actions in Libya began at a certain start date, albeit Bush and Rice made new in roads in the earlier part of this decade that may have contributed to what Obama has implemented to date. Such was not true for Vietnam, seeing that the U.S. entered that war incrementally, in a series of steps between 1950 and 1965. President Harry S. Truman, in May 1950, authorized economic and military aid to the French, who were fighting to retain control of their Indochina colony, which was comprised of Laos, Cambodia and Vietnam.

But the Vietnamese Nationalist defeated French forces at Dienbienphu in 1954, which led the French to create a non-Communist entity south of that line. Since the United States refused to accept this, President Dwight D. Eisenhower went into nation building mode that became South Vietnam. Similar to what the US and NATO are doing with taking the sides of the rebels in Libya.

Although not on the record, like then, we and other nations have sent military advisers to help the country's rebels. Thus far to date, the NATO no-fly zone has failed to both protect citizens and aid the rebels; each similar to our first entrance into Vietnam where we intervened in the middle of civil war. The reason we lost in Vietnam was due to not having lucid goals and objectives and a lack of confidence in our mission in southeastern Asia. The same can be asserted for the current Libya policy where we have no goal and worse, do not even know who we are supporting.

What is evident is eerily similar to 1961, when President John F. Kennedy secretly sent 400 Green Beret soldiers to teach the South Vietnamese how to fight against Communist guerrillas in South Vietnam. By the time of his death in November 1963, there were more 16,000 U.S. military advisers in South Vietnam.

The lesson that Obama and our politicians should take is that history is the best teacher. After Kennedy was killed and Lyndon Johnson began became president, the incessant bombing of North Vietnam increased and Johnson sent the Marines to South Vietnam in 1965. Although Johnson had intended to fight a limited war, he did not expect that the North Vietnamese would be able to hold out long against the American military.

To date our air campaign has had little effect against Muammar Qaddafi. If we make the mistake of assuming that airpower will get him out singularly, we are wrong and may be in line for a long term stalemate. It is also strange that after all these years have passed since we first jumped into Vietnam, we have yet to figure out policy which match our political and military goals under such circumstances. It baffles the mind, doesn't it?

10

These gas prices are kicking all of us in the rear end. Many blame the president, others commodity market speculators, and still others OPEC. They all are off from the way I see this issue. The real issue and the culprit is the U.S. dollar, specifically its reduced value and purchasing power.

It seems almost intentional. The avoiding discussing the declining value of the dollar as it relates to the pricing increases we are seeing in everything from oil to food to gas. Politicians seem to just want to exploit the issue by appealing to popular sentiment. The fact is that the U.S. dollar continues to hit record lows against all major foreign currencies especially the yuan, the euro, and the yen. Add to that the recent IMF findings that China's economy will surpass that of America in 2016, it is more than meets the eye when speaking about the rising cost of gas. Why? Because we are not going through a recovery as the government suggest but rather a debt spending boom based on the home buying explosion of years past.

The truth is that U.S. household debt reached a high in June of $8.7 trillion, and with rising unemployment and no economic growth, it is reflected in the reduced value of the dollar. Such negatively impacts U.S. treasuries, especially now since the Japanese government will need to sell its U.S. treasuries to deal with and pay for cleaning up and rebuilding after the earthquake. Add to this gumbo China, which has the largest dollar surplus in the world, who saw its foreign exchange re-

22

serves increased by 197.4 billion U.S. dollars in the first three months of this year to 3.04 trillion by the end of March.

Now back to oil and gas. In simple terms, the weakness in the U.S. dollar is causing everything to go up. This is happening in an environment in which the rate of new debt growth among families is growing and the overall U.S. manufacturing economy declines. This inherently impacts the dollar since what politicians ignore in their budget and deficit battles is the fact that U.S. trade deficits and the dollar system are connected.

Historically, in 1944 the Bretton Woods agreement solidified the dollar as the preeminent world reserve currency, defining the dollar in value to be 1/35th of an ounce of gold. In 1971, when President Nixon refused to pay out any of our remaining 280 million ounces of gold, he made the dollar what is today, fiat currency.

Oil is a critical economic and strategic resource and since it is traded in U.S. dollars, when the dollar weakens, in terms of any other major foreign currency, the countries exporting oil get less. Thus when the dollar goes down in buying power they ask for more dollars for every barrel of oil. This gets even trickier since there is no shortage of oil via production currently. What they is clear is that just a decade ago the U.S. economy was three times the size of China's. In contrast and by current estimates China's economy will expand from $11.2 trillion this year to $19 trillion in 2016, while the U.S. economy will rise from $15.2 trillion to $18.8 trillion.

23

All I am trying to say is that the America we once knew with the all powerful dollar bill isn't the same. The fact is that we have a surplus of oil we are not refining. In addition, what we are seeing is the impact of a weakened dollar on oil demand in non-dollar economies. Oil producers sell their products in dollars. The dollars they get are used to buy other stuff around the globe. If it cost them more dollars to do so then they have to sell their oil for more dollars.

As long as the U.S. dollar is continuously devalued (inflated) by Federal Reserve and U.S. government monetary policies, oil producing nations will lose money if they don't raise the price.

The problem is our government and our monetary policies. The dollar may never be the same. Yet, all the time wall street, big oil companies, and politicians are getting richer as they sell all that made America great away to corporations and other nations through our monetary policy. Yep, that's America; the greatest and best government money can buy.

11

It is strange how things come full circle. Cartesian mathematics could not have had a better postulate for the circle than Obama's terse maneuvers to take out the aging and dialysis requiring Osama Bin Laden. During the election, Obama made it clear that he was not opposed to all wars but rather Iraq was not a battle that targeted Al Qaeda. He made it clear that, if elected, he would focus on both Afghanistan and Pakistan. John McCain ridiculed him for adding Pakistan as his main focus.

Obama's announcement that Bin Laden was killed in Pakistan, occurred just two years into his Presidency, successfully keeping his promise to capture and kill America's public enemy number one.

Obama has always been underestimated by the GOP even when for 8 years, Bush falsely elevated terror alert levels to provide a fake penumbra that the safety of America was priority number one. Especially when we consider that the Bush administration was warned by the CIA on Monday, August 6, 2001, that attacks by Al Qaeda were imminent and he did nothing about it. The GOP incessantly suggest that democrats are "soft" on terrorism, while the bloodiest attack on this country since Pearl Harbor happened on the GOP's watch. Also recall how the Bush administration, swiftly flew members of the Bin Laden family out of the country before they could be questioned. Yes, how quick we are to remember that OBL was a member of the Saudi Royal family. I will not even introduce how Bush pulled our military out of Tora Bora when they were within an inch of capturing bin Laden.

Obama has even taken it from the left when he vowed to escalate the fight in Afghanistan – a tactic that placed more pressure on bin Laden. He alone directed Panetta to make it a priority to get Osama and personally authorized the hit.

Obama has has a great week: he put the birther movement to shame, visited the tornado ravaged south, and was a star at the Whitehouse comedy gala this past weekend. Yes he has been vindicated. The query now is if he will use this to withdraw our troops from Afghanistan and cut our military budget, and save Medicare and our economy.

I hope not with regard to the first part and would like to see him use this same model in Yemen to get American-born Anwar Al-Awlak. The president has demonstrated that actions speak louder than words. While Trump and the Birthers were looking for a birth certificate and threatening to close own the federal government, Obama looked for and found bin Laden and kept it a secret with his stellar poker face.

12

If one has followed President Obama's statements and position on the Middle East and North Africa prior to his policy speech on the region last week you, like me, probably have no clue to the reasoning behind his words. After reading his remarks last Wednesday I am in even more of a stupor of consternation.

What I can say is that his approach and policy alike are whimsical or fickle at best and unprincipled and inconsistent at worse – thus the rarefied stupor I alluded to previously. For example, I recall how initially in Egypt he proclaimed his support for Hosni Mubarak in word, but fleetingly altered this position upon the observation that President Mubarak did not have the support of the military. Similarly, in Bahrain, he offered effeminate words of support for the long ruling leadership yet at the same time he attempted to protect the leadership and longtime alley for the sake of the fleet anchored in its harbor. Even as the Monarch, with the aid of Saudi tanks and military, killed unarmed protesters, the administration and its figure head turned a blind eye to the citizenry desire for democratic rule and liberty. This same behavior and action drew harsh military reprisals and words from Obama via NATO requesting Muammar el-Qaddafi leave office.

In Libya, our military are protecting the innocent, but we do no such protection for those in Yemen, Syria, or Bahrain. In his speech, Obama commented, that "humiliation takes place every day in many parts of the world – the relentless tyranny of governments that deny their citizens dignity". He added "we can, and will speak out for a set of core principles – principles that have guided our response to the events over the past six months. In fact the President alludes to hearing the calls for help, but strangely it is only in the Middle East and Libya but no other parts of Africa.

The problem for me is that there is no one stated standard nor any unifying principle that guides this new policy. This means that any effective policy for unstable governments on our behalf will require coherence, which thus far is lacking. Will he treat all attacks on the general populations the same? Will King Abdullah of Saudi be held to the same standard of Qaddafi? What makes a distinction to have different positions between Qaddafi and Syria's president Bashar al-Assad? He did not even mention Bahrain or Saudi Arabia in his speech.

The Obama administration is all over the place, to say we hear the calls for democracy yet cover our ears from similar cries from the Congo, Uganda, Sudan and other nations is disingenuous and fails the litmus test of reality and consistency.

Halfway around the world, another fine foreign policy mess is manifesting its head thanks to Bill Clinton, George W. Bush, and Barack Obama. In the name of emotion and in the form of terror American-backed warlords in Somalia have free reign to destroy a nation from its infrastructure to its government in a vain effort to persecute the Union of Islamic Courts (UIC), who they consider terrorist affiliates of Al Qaeda, a group that once held warlords at bay, who established order, stopped the open dealing of drugs and even allowed Freedom of speech. That is until the United States intervened and made Somalia into another front in the global "War on Terror". Now the country has returned to the mess prior to U.S. foreign policy intervention which has seen individual clans battling for their piece of the Somalia pie. The United States and U.S. policy makers have never had a valid and viable understanding regarding the troubles confronting Somali society. Ignorance was not enough for the United States, as part of the international community, under the auspices of Somalia humanitarian operations to make things even worse. U.S. efforts assisted in debilitating starvation and saving many lives, but we couldn't stop there and decided to wave our magical military wand and engender a backwards slide into disorder and anarchy.

After all of our wasted economic support in this effort now what we thought we were attempting to prevent is coming to fruition – a mad dash and violent battles by warlords and tribal clans to collect as much land as possible. We have engendered more instability and corruption in the nation. It is like we never thought what could occur if all of the Islamic insurgents were to be defeated and left the region.

The failures in Somalia reflect U.S. foreign policy at its best – inept and destructive. Yet we still appear to have not learned from the lessons of Somalia. In theory, American interest in the Horn of Africa region dates back to the Cold War when both the Soviet Union and the United States competed to gain allies and influence in Africa and elsewhere throughout the world. Consequently, it was another comedy of errors that reflected more on our self-centeredness than trying to get a nation to solve its own problems internally. This is because in the U.S. ignorance of the tribalism of Somali culture was a major shortcoming before and during our intervention in the African nation. We entered Somalia in December 1992 under the guise of stopping the starvation of hundreds of thousands of people. Although it succeeded in this mission, the chaotic political situation eventually demonstrated a poorly organized nation-building operation in that merely increased hostility toward us and our interest as a nation.

Today it is estimated that more than 20 mini-states comprise Somalia. What was holding the nation together prior to our intervention exist no longer and it has become a country fragmented and although we attempted to end starvation, we have only made human suffering in the drought-stricken country worse. Moreover, this blunder is off the radar of main stream media for some reason or another. Maybe we really don't or didn't have the humanitarian interest of Africans in our hearts in the first place. I think the adamantine Laurel and

29

Hardy said it best, "this is another fine mess you've gotten us into".

14

Hypocrisy is a noun that in essence means to act on the stage and to purport to be what one is not or to believe what one is not. Its modern form is a combination of Greek and old French. This is the best word I can use to illustrate the position of the United States and the Obama administration with respect to their blatant efforts to block a vote on the addition of Palestine to the United Nations.

I find it awkwardly detached and unusual for this administration in particular, given a fitted and able discernment of the president's address at the American University in Cairo. During that address he stated, "I have come here to seek a new beginning between the United States and Muslims around the world; one based upon mutual interest and mutual respect; and one based upon the truth that America and Islam are not exclusive, and need not be in competition. Instead, they overlap, and share common principles - principles of justice and progress; tolerance and the dignity of all human beings".

These were words stated by President Barack Obama during his address to the American University at Cairo some two minutes into his address. It took him some six more pages before he said, "it is also undeniable that the Palestinian people, Muslims and Christians, have suffered in pursuit of a homeland. For more than sixty years they have endured the pain of dislocation. Many wait in refugee camps in the West Bank, Gaza, and neighboring lands for a life of peace and security that they have never been able to lead. They endure the daily humiliations, large and small, that come with occupation. So let there be no doubt: the situation for the Palestinian people is intolerable. America will not turn our backs on the legitimate Palestinian aspiration for dignity, opportunity, and a state of their own.

This threat to veto the vote may serve to destroy any attempt for a desire to serve two terms for the president and worse, increase future attacks against the U.S. by radical fanatics. Obama's cabal, under the auspices of Secretary of State Hillary Clinton in concert with Tony Blair's special envoy to the region, and EU Foreign Policy Chief Catherine Ashton, has manifested itself in a last ditch effort of brinkmanship to block the Palestinian Authority's desire for a vote in the United Nations General Assembly to recognize an independent state of Palestine. The result will be a diplomatic and political disaster for the president, the democrats and any effort to win a second term at the executive level, especially since by all accounts, the resolution will pass by a large margin, without support from the U.S., and a few other nations. It is strange since it was Obama, who in his Sept. 23, 2010 address to the General Assembly, originally raised the goal of admitting Palestine to the UN by September 2011.

Obama continues to say that an Israeli-Palestinian peace agreement is one of his highest priorities, yet he has made less progress toward Israeli-Palestinian peace than any administration since the early 1970's.

This sets a major problem in motion for Obama and his plans to seek re-election if the Jewish vote turns against him, especially given the recent special elections in New York's 9th district in which a republican won for the first time since the turn of the century. The loss in Tuesday's special election for the seat formerly held by Rep. Anthony Weiner (D-N.Y.) may "send a message" to President Obama concerning his administration's stance on Israel. This was not from a republican but rather Rep. Eliot Engel (D-N.Y.). Not to mention that it was former Mayor Ed Koch (D) who called on voters to back the republican businessman in order to send a message to Obama about his Israel policy. Mayor Koch disagrees with Obama's view that Israel's pre-1967 borders should be the baseline for Middle East peace talks. Thus, the administration's insistence on trying to persuade Israel to stop building settlements, without success in concert with the aforementioned equals an effrontery to the American Jewish community.

Sen. John Barrasso (R-Wyo.) has indicated his concern regarding the Palestinian Authority's (PA) bid for the United Nation's (UN) to recognize their statehood. Barrasso wants the U.S. to immediately stop funds it sends to the PA annually as well as the UN if statehood is recognized. Then there is Sen. Marco Rubio, republican from Florida who says if the vote in the United Nations to create a Palestinian state is successful, it would set back the Middle East peace process and would only add to the regional turmoil and instability. Not only is the concern by republicans and the pro-Zionist lobby problematic, but similar concerns have been brought to fruition by Arab states. Saudi Arabia has expressed outrage for Palestinians to many members of Congress, a congress that in voice supports what has occurred in Egypt, Libya, and Tunisia but against such in Palestine

Not only has the president been unsuccessful in his efforts to broker a peace agreement between Israel and Palestine, now he seemingly has lost one of his major political allies. The concern is that after dealing several defeating blows to terrorism through the deaths of major Al Qaeda leaders, he may be stoking the flames for more attacks from individuals who take his flip flop on the issue of Palestinian statehood as a reason to lash out against the United States again.

The veto in the UN may help save Obama a major voting constituency, however, the question remains, how will this be perceived in the Arab world and if winning an election by any means necessary is more important than ensuring our safety from future terroristic attacks in the future?

15

The first time I read about it, I doubted its truth on historical and political merits alone. Not saying it was not true, but rather it was questionable with respect to the aforementioned and its timely manifestation. I am referring to the recent and weird allegation made suggesting that Iran was behind a plot to assassinate Adel al Jubeir and bomb the Israeli embassy. According to U.S. Attorney General Eric Holder, the plot was "directed and approved by elements of the Iranian government and, specifically, senior members of the Quds Force". But the catch is that according to U.S. officials, the suspect would pay

$1.5 million to the Los Zetas drug cartel to kill the Saudi ambassador at a Washington restaurant also frequented by congressmen and senators.

I have written in this very forum about the U.S. and Iran, most recently as it concerned our inability to be consistent with our positions taken concerning how we decided who should be ousted and what citizenry we supported during the unrest in the Middle East and North Africa starting with Tunisia last year and more specifically, how we tend to look the other way in Saudi Arabia and Bahrain but not Libya or Uganda. Not to mention the taciturn neglect the current administration shows to African Americans while kowtowing to the American Zionist lobby.

Our own history should have the less than average reader concerned about our allegations concerning this plot. First, we should be reminded that the U.S. government gave Saddam Hussein biological weapons and urged him to use them against Iran. Although Hussein decided that biological weapons went too far and backed down from the U.S. plan, we used the same biological weapons we gave to Hussein as a basis to invade Iraq, even though UN monitors had already verified that the weapons had been destroyed.

Then there was the recent fiasco in which we provided support and approval for Israel to assassinate several leading Iranian nuclear scientist over the past two years in an attempt to impede Iran's progression toward nuclear self sufficiency. As if I am actually supposed to believe that Iran is a threat to us.

We are just another bouncer under the auspice of a new administrative head. We already fund Israel's military, why should we fight wars for them as well? Maybe it is a ploy to take some heat away from Eric Holder is getting slammed for the illegal "fast and furious" gun running activities. After all, who else to better assert that Iran tried to recruit a Mexican drug cartel to kill the ambassador of Saudi Arabia via a weed smoking used car salesman from Texas than Holder? Maybe it is a way for us to justify the Obama administrations giving cluster bombs to Israel just a week after former New York mayor Ed Koch stated openly that Obama was no friend of Israel.

Maybe Iranian parliament member Alaeddin Boroujerdi was right when he said the accusation was "a plot to divert the public opinion from the crisis Obama is grappling with". Plus the informant is dubious to say the least seeing he was "previously charged in connection with narcotics offenses...in exchange for... various narcotics investigations" being dismissed. This was based on the indictment of course.

The case made by the U.S is more media PR than actual fact since they are not supported by any hard evidence. The only evidence we have, which isn't even related to this adduced collusion is the history of our relationship with this Persian nation - the only Persian nation in the world who happens to be surrounded by nations who hate Persians. Also they are the only Shia run regime in the world, surrounded by regimes that hate Shia. True they are a major producer of oil, but still have to import gasoline.

My question is why the suspect would even ask if the others involved were "any good with explosives?" We know that the US Intelligence indicates Iran's Quds Force are the best in the world when it comes to improvised explosive devices and explosively formed penetrators into Iraq. It seems as if Obama wants to show Israel we will do anything for them even start a war with Iran. As well it seems that we have been doing all in our might to fabricate a reason for such a war just to appease the Israel lobby. The only query that remains is why now and I suspect we will be finding out more real soon. I am skeptical seeing this is the week we have a massive airlift drill in the Mediterranean with Saudi Arabia and Israel.

16

Is it just me, or is it strangely funny and coincidental that over the past decade everywhere we sent US troops in which we aided in the death; killing or assignation of a sovereign foreign head of state has been in an energy rich country with vast amounts of oil and/or natural gas. Saddam Hussein was in Iraq and he was hanged. Kaddafi was in Libya and he was summarily executed. In Afghanistan, no telling how many tribal and regional leaders (since they historically never had a nation state with a central government) we have killed. And as I stated in each case they have what we need to paraphrase the great Biz Markie – oil and natural gas. This tradition is continuing with the recent deployment of U.S. service personnel to Uganda. oil and Uganda? Yes.

If you didn't know Uganda is sitting on tons of oil. Oil exploration began in Uganda's northwestern Lake Albert basin nearly a decade ago and according to estimates by the Energy Ministry, the African nation has over two billion barrels of oil. The British firm Tullow Oil operates three oil blocks in the region, and had sold off part of its stake to Total and China's CNOOC. But the sale was halted following the allegations of bribery. Specifically that Prime Minister Amama Mbabazi has been accused of receiving funds to lobby for oil production rights on behalf of the Italian oil firm ENI, which eventually lost its bid for exploration rights to British firm Tullow Oil. In addition, Foreign Affairs Minister Sam Kutesa and Internal Affairs Minister Hilary Onek have also been accused of taking bribes from Tullow Oil worth over US$23 million and $8 million respectively.

As a result of these activities occurring over the past few weeks, it is ironic the Obama has decided to intervene with the rebels he claims are wrecking havoc in the region and fostering social unrest. Obama notified House Speaker John Boehner, of deploying the mostly Special Operations Forces, to central Africa with the first troops reportedly arriving in Uganda on last Wednesday.

Truth is that the rebels are representative of the people just as those he sent NATO forces to protect in Libya. It was hoped that the discovery of oil would improve the economic conditions of the masses of which 51 percent of the population lives below the poverty line. The Uganda economy is suffering from a 20-year high double-digit inflation now at 28.3 percent.

Oil exploration began in Uganda's northwestern Lake Albert basin nearly a decade ago, with initial strikes being made in 2006 and is scheduled to begin oil refining in 2014 . The 2.5 billion barrels of crude along Uganda's western border with Congo will be extracted upon the development of a refinery in a phased manner, starting with capacity of around 40,000-60,000 barrels a day before peaking at 150,000 barrels a day by 2016.

Many are unaware that Africa's exports of oil to the United States, largely from Nigeria and the dictator state of Equatorial Guinea, at rates almost equal to those of the Middle East. But again why now? I have outlined several factors including the suggestion of US intervention by, the International Crisis Group, which is the principal author of "Responsibility to Protect," the military doctrine used by Obama to justify the U.S. led NATO campaign in Libya. Even more coincidental is that billionaire George Soros is a member of its executive board and personally, just recently recommended the U.S. deploy a special advisory military team to Uganda.

Soros, via his Open Society Institute is one of only three nongovernmental funders of the Global Centre for Responsibility to Protect, as well as other Institute advisors including Samantha Power, the National Security Council special adviser to Obama on human rights, who also aided in the establishment of the International Criminal Court. Soros himself maintains close ties to oil interests in Uganda. As early as April of 2010, Soros' International Crisis Group, or ICG, released a report sent to the White House and other lawmakers advising the U.S. military to run special operations in Uganda to seek Kony's capture. It makes sense seeing that in 2008 a

National Oil and Gas Policy, proposed with aid from a Soros-funded group, was supposed to be a general road map for the handling and use of the oil.

Like in Libya, the U.S. mission will be to advise forces seeking to kill or capture Joseph Kony, the leader of the rebel Lord's Resistance Army (LRA). In the past, the Obama administration has stated it would only deploy U.S. troops in the Middle East, Africa or Central Asia to target terrorist groups and rogue states that threaten the U.S. Unfortunately this is not an apt description of the Lord's Resistance Army

So why is it that all of a sudden we are sending troops to another African nation? Not any nation but one rich in oil? We know the region, which includes South Sudan - which became an independent state in July after a two-decade civil war with the government in Khartoum, is also one of the emerging oil-rich states producing 500,000 barrels per day. This account for 80 percent of the country's untapped oil deposits: meaning our presence may provide for increased penetration by Western-based oil firms in the United States and Europe. We know that the U.S. was a major proponent of splitting off South Sudan from the central government, as well as supporting the secessionist rebel movements in the western region of Darfur.

South Sudan became an independent state in July after a two-decade civil war with the government in Khartoum. Sudan is one of the emerging oil-rich states producing 500,000 barrels per day. The oil concessions in Sudan were largely in partnership with the People's Republic of China and other Asian and Middle Eastern states.

Uganda has yet to produce a single barrel of oil, but it is obvious that its presence has played a key role in the Obama's administration via the influence of George Soros to intervene militarily to help Uganda fight the rebels of the LRA who are currently in the Central African Republic.

I find this puzzling since we had these opportunities before oil was found and neglected to get involved. Now we are and the only fact that has changed is that the country is now rich in oil and we want to get out hands on it. To do such, we will most likely kill another person in another nation who has the support to the people more than the elected government does.

17

I often wonder what Obama's father would say about his son's incessant intervention in Africa. For certain, I know he would not say Obama's loves him some Africa. Maybe he would because every time we look around, he sending troops to the continent left and right and in all cases to date, to murder established leaders. We saw what his intervention in Libya resulted in and we know that the goal in Uganda is to kill Joseph Kony, the leader of the rebel Lord's Resistance Army (LRA). And in Somalia, a nation that has not had a functioning government since 1991 when warlords overthrew former dictator Mohamed Siad Barre, we may be doing our dirtiest job.

Mohammed Siad Barre came to power via a military coup in October 1969 scientific socialism as Somali state policy - Somali nationalism with the goal of uniting all Somali people under one flag. Once (1970s), the United State provided military and economic assistance to Somalia, and the U.S. Embassy in Mogadishu became one of the biggest American diplomatic missions in Africa. After being criticized by the world for providing military support to the Siad Barre regime, efforts in Congress to cut off military assistance to Somali finally succeeded in 1989.

Although we know that the present food and refugee emergency in Somalia is considered to be the worst humanitarian crisis in the world, placing millions at immediate risk via disease, drought and massive starvation, the Obama administration sent a U.S. Marine task force to the region instead of focusing on humanitarian aid and has escalated drone attacks in Somalia that contribute even more to the starvation and death of additional millions of Africans. For it is the administrations belief that the al-Shabab resistance is mostly responsible for the drought emergency.

Strange since the Obama administration has put in place policies to limit food aid to the region in an effort to starve out those who might be supporting the Shabab. Yes food as a weapon of war in Somalia. What we forget is that the problems of today can be connected to our action four years ago when we got the Ethiopian government to invade Somalia in an effort to overthrow an Islamist government that had established peace by ended street battles between warlords and militias via Islamic fundamentalist law..

But what is more problematic for me as an African American who has lived in the region (Ethiopia in 1999) and visited Somalia, is the reckless manner in which we disrespect and lessen the value of lives there via the US policy of using drones or unmanned aerial vehicles (UAVs) to kill civilians in the hundreds daily. In addition, this is not even mentioned on the news nor is discussed openly by President Obama almost Bush-like. Maybe this is why the President is seeking to ban the access of international news agencies the likes of Press TV who reports such daily.

When I lived in Africa, Press TV, BBC, Der Welt Television (Germany) and Al-Jazerra were watched more than any American News outlet and to me are equal to ITN and PBS in their coverage of world news. Since I do not have cable television, I am left to reading the web sites of these respected news agencies. Case in point, the information I have found on the aforementioned in the past two weeks alone is startling and unbeknownst to most US citizens.

On Oct 14, 2001, an attack by a U.S. UAV resulted in the killing of at least 78 people and injured 64 others in southern Somalia. The attack, which occurred near Qooqani town located in southern Somalia happened the same day another US drone attack killed 11 civilians and wounded 34 more in Hoosingow district in the south of the country. Oct 21, 2001 another attack by a US unmanned aerial vehicle killed at least 44 civilians and injured 63 others in southern Somalia near Ras Kamboni town in the Badhaadhe district of Lower Juba region near the border with Kenya. Several hours later, a US done attack killed 22 in Kudhaa Island in southern Somalia near the border with Kenya.

Somali military officials reported an attack on Oct 22, 2011 near the town of Bilis Qooqani, an unmanned US drone strike killed at least 49 people in famine-stricken in southern Somalia, while injuring at least 68 others. The next day, Oct 23, 2011, US drones carried out attacks near the Bilis Qooqani districts in southern Somalia, leaving 9 dead and 14 others wounded.

The following day, On Oct 24, 2011, an attack took place in the Somali island of Kudhaa near the country's border with Kenya according to Somali army officer Colonel Aden Dheere in which killed at least 36 Somali people. Later that day, another 59 people were killed and dozens more injured during French military attacks on Kudhaa.

In each case Washington claims the airstrikes target militants, though most such attacks have resulted in civilian casualties in Somalia. More recently representatives of the Obama administration have denied any "US involved or supported airstrikes in Somalia: a claim friends and associates of mine from my days living in the region contradict.

Whatever the case, the facts remain the same. First, Somalia strategic location in the horn of Africa and its vast natural resources cannot be questioned. Second, it is not implausible that the U.S. would do anything to keep China, India and Russia out of the region. Third, the nation is a geopolitical prize that has brought about the United States via the Obama administration to use neocolonial approaches to develop a foothold in the nation as well as offers a reason to employ resources of the U.S. Africa Command (AFRICOM), to achieve any clandestine objectives, especially in the context of the Trans-Sahara Counter Terrorism Partnership (TSCTP). Supported by the U.S. Africa Command (USAFRICOM) and the Special Operations Command (SOCAFRICA). Not to mention they are involved with assisting the brother of President Yoweri Museveni in training troops for military efforts both in Somalia and Uganda. Strange since the Obama administration as recently as yesterday denied any involvement in arial strikes in Somalia. Like I said, very Bush-like.

18

America is dead. Yes we are basically attending the wake of our once great nation. I wanted to hold off before I wrote this but this week sent me over the edge. I realized this when the situation at Penn State and Dr. Conrad Murray's trial were headlining most news outlets like they were actually that important. I had an inkling that this was the case when they started leading with Herman Cain's alleged sexual miscues, but the Penn State fiasco made it all clearer.

As a people we do not have the intellectual capacity to put things in perspective. I know molesting kids is wrong but it would still be just as heinous if it was done by a teacher at a local school and doesn't warrant being on TV as the first story, equally to the Dr. Murray and Cain mess as if it is really important on the problems we are confronting as a nation today. Even worse is that we do not have the foresight to even question why such is on each day and worse, question ourselves why we don't.

It is almost magical, just a few days after the brutal execution and solemnization of Col. Mumar Gaddafi, there has been little word about the nation. Likewise, there has also been a reduction of the coverage regarding the atrocities of what is occurring daily in Syria. Why this is is my query and as such I have a few suggestions I would like to offer in support of my observations. I may even throw in a little Israel into the mix for good measure.

Seems like it was clear from the start, Obama and US higher ups (corporations) had a desire to see Gaddafi out of the picture. So much so that the same higher ups had Obama do their bidding by asking the UN war with Libya, Barack Obama's administration is breaking new ground. Obtaining a U.N. Security Council resolution has legitimated U.S. bombing raids under international law. But the U.N. Charter is not a substitute for the U.S. Constitution, which gives Congress, not the president, the power "to declare war."

My question is what make Libya different from Syria, and why has the Present administration said nothing about either? I mean constitutionality we had no authority for our Libyan intervention, since Libya did not attack our "armed forces." Why not do the same for Syria? It is obvious the President doesn't need the support of congress to do such since, in the Libyan case; the president had plenty of time to get congressional support.

Maybe the reason we no longer mention Libya in media outlets is because of the results. We already see horrifying reprisals from the US-backed rebels against their political opponents given their incessant killing of each other as well as supporters of the previous regime. Not to mention that the civilian toll from NATO bombs grew albeit they were supposed to be protecting a civilian population. Obama stated that his actions in Libya were "in the national security and foreign policy interests of the United States, pursuant to my constitutional authority to conduct U.S. foreign relations and as Commander in Chief and Chief Executive."

True, Obama has called for Syrian President Bashar al-Assad is an ally of Iran, foe of Israel and sponsor of the armed militant group Hezbollah, to leave office but that is about it. Although Assad and his ruling circle are members of the minority Alawite sect, which makes up about 12 percent of Syria's population, Obama has not even asked the UN or NATO to intervene to protect civilians there. There were no massacres taking place in Libya before the NATO attack but they are occurring in Syria.

All I can say is that the President has shown himself to be more neo-conservative than any neo-conservative and seems to use "regime change" just as much as George W. Bush and his inner circle. Now he has extended this purview by ending US funding of the U.N. Educational, Scientific and Cultural Organization (UNESCO) after they held a vote to approve the Palestinian Authority's full membership in the agency.

What is all of this for? Is it to appease Israel; is it to show he is in charge prior to 2012? I cannot say but I will assert that it is more of the political same – WAGGING THE

DOG. By this I mean "When something of secondary importance improperly takes on the role of something of primary importance."

Truth is that Obama tends to foreign policy because he is lost in what to don domestically. I cannot figure out why it is important for him to make it easier for foreign corporations to invest in American than American corporations to invest here at home. While abroad we see what has happened in Europe and know that the head of China's biggest ratings agency, Dagong Global Credit Rating, is warning that it may downgrade the U.S.'s sovereign debt rating again because of Washington's failure to tackle the federal budget deficit. Why can't he do our business in the same manner he does for his wealthy doors?

Over the last year, the Obama administration aggressively pushed a $433-million plan to buy an experimental smallpox drug, although we do not need such or don't even know if the drug will work. What we do know is that the no-bid contract went to New York-based Siga Technologies Inc.; a company who's a major share holder is billionaire and a longtime Democratic Party donor. Ronald O. Perelman.

I just do not get it. Our national debt is almost 15 trillion dollars, if you include interest it's almost 55 trillion dollars, making my of this debt is just under $175,000. And if you didn't know Mr. President, my personal value and net worth is shrinking while you're folk on Capital hill's is growing. The collective net worth of all of the members of Congress increased by 25 percent between 2008 and 2010.

Just help me understand and I will have your back, otherwise I will call it like I see it, that from the White House to the congress there is sciolism on both sides of the aisle and in the hood too, since most folks too dumb to think or look for themselves and would prefer to attend to who Herman Cain tried to get give him fellatio allegedly, or how many little boys a perverted coach has molested.

19

Unlike some folks, I remember the day the people of Iran overthrew the Shah of Iran in 1979. Looking at our current contrived grievance with Iran, I wonder if our current administration does. Over the past year, due to the omnipotent pressure and power of the U.S. Zionist lobby, we have seen multiple military attacks on Iran nuclear facilities and even the kidnapping and assassination of leading Iranian academics and scientist. We have even seen pressure placed on democrats by this lobby in particular, the loss of the New York 9th district congressional seat vacated by Anthon Weiner, to such an extent that the present administration sent bunker buster bombs to Israel to appease their supporter. In fact just this New Year, Obama signed into law sanctions against Iran oil exports. I guess it was designed to show America's Jewish lobby and Israel that we are hard on Iran.

I have been taking my time writing on this because I want to see how all the chips fall. Just last week Treasury Secretary Timothy F. Geithner attempted to get Chinese policy makers to join an American-led campaign to reduce oil exports from Iran because of its nuclear program. However, like Russia, they have rejected to participate in the US/European sanctions or the oil embargo directed toward the Persian nation. This will be problematic since it will be the Treasury Department responsibility to enforce sanction laws, especially given that the new legislation, which would prevent access by nations who do not support sanctions on Iran to the American financial system. Although loop holes in the law allow for selected exemptions, in all honestly, I do not think that the President, just as presidents past, is ready for this may proffer in an election year or to our economy. Currently, China's trade surplus with the United States widened 24.2 percent to $17.4 billion in December.

China exports $1.5 trillion of its production and ships 20% of its exports to the U.S., which created a $252 billion trade deficit in 2010. Not to mention that as of last year China owned $1.16 trillion in U.S. debt in the form of Treasury bills, notes and bonds - 26% of the total of $4.5 trillion held by the public. Consequently, this makes China America's largest banker, giving it leverage over the US as evident when China threatens to sell part of its holdings whenever the U.S. pressures it to raise the value of the yuan. It is no wonder that the U.S. trade deficit with China in 2010 was 27 times larger than it was back in 1990.

Another concern is that some fear Russia fears Israel is pushing America to war on Iran "which could retaliate by blocking" Persian Gulf oil shipments. It is clear that Russia will do what it perceives as necessary to protect its strategically important Tartus, Syria base, its only Mediterranean one (there is as we speak a Russian aircraft carrier battle group is positioned nearby). Then we have 15,000 combat troops in Kuwait, inclusive of two Army infantry brigades and a helicopter unit along with two aircraft carrier battle groups remains in the region.

19

It is clear that the Obama policy is another political divertissement of imperious old men who have never been to war and like to say they have a right to prevent other nations from self determination, especially when it comes to developing nuclear power. Even it is in the form of weapons, history shows that the only folk who have used nuclear weapons have been the United States. So important is this that we will assist in the assignation of scientist – an act that if implemented by the Taliban or Iranians we would call terroristic. Now we have even indicated to them that any effort to control their own geopolitical borders via the Strait of Hormuz would evoke a swift response from the U.S. military. France's Le Figaro said "the U.S. and Israel have carried out multiple acts of sabotage against sensitive nuclear installations, while ordering targeted killings of Iranian nuclear experts." Meaning that both Israeli and U.S. recruit Iranian assets to sabotage Iran's nuclear program, "which includes targeted assassinations of Iranian nuclear experts...."Again strange since we say one reason we are hard on Iran is because they are a vehicle for state sponsored terrorism.

As it stands, Obama will likely find some excuse to save face, and maybe even attack Iran. As we speak, he is trying to gain support from Middle East allies in preparation for an impending U.S.-Iranian confrontation. This is hard to understand for two reasons. First, we just got out of Iraq and are trying to get out of Afghanistan, why do we want another war so soon with a country of 75 million in which historically, sanctions have never worked. Moreover we as a nation cannot distance our self from targeted assassinations and other subversion in Iran.

He may as well give up on any support from China and when they and Russia do not go along, he will have do-do on his face because he will be powerless to do anything against them: Russia could damage our economy by artificially raising the price of crude oil and China by stop purchasing our debt and/or selling US papers in bulk causing more devaluation of the dollar. I hope the Obama administration thinks this out, for every indication suggest that Washington, Israel and NATO allies cannot wait to bump heads with Iran and Syria. This even when the fact remains that no evidence whatever suggests an Iranian nuclear weapons program, according to the latest March 2011 US intelligence assessment.

It is strange since while the White House is plotting against Tehran, the living standards of the American working class continue to fall. According to Reuters, 23.7 million American workers are either unemployed or underemployed right now. I can figure out why spending billions on another military effort (war) is more important than spending that money here at home where it is needed.

20

With each passing day, the Obama administration and the international community appear to be struggling to find a way to deal with the crisis in Syria. Just four days ago the United States closed the U.S. embassy in Syria after Russia and China blocked a UN resolution drafted by Arab and European countries on Saturday that may have supplied aid or set up a buffer zone that would involve a military dimension to protect vulnerable civilians.

U.S. Secretary of State Hillary Clinton called the veto a "travesty" and Washington's U.N. ambassador Susan Rice said she was "disgusted" by Russia and China's vetoes adding that "any further bloodshed that flows will be on their hands." President Barack Obama's asked for the U.N. Security Council to hold firm against the Syrian regime's "relentless brutality" and has indicated that the ongoing conflict in Syria should be resolved without foreign military interference, suggesting that a solution for Syria can be proffered via negotiations.

The problem for the president is twofold. First the position and inconsistencies his policy has manifest throughout the democratic uprisings in the region from Egypt to Libya and the appearance that his cabinet officials could send a strong message of accountability and/or his perceived lack of desire to hold his senior appointees responsible for their performance.

The entire situation in the Middle East is untenable in its present state. From the current inaction and war of words, it is almost as if the Obama administration sees the real targets of the Syria regime-change goal as Russia and China, since both see the U.S. as seeking to establish absolute control over the strategic oil supplies in the Persian Gulf. Not to mention that human rights advocates view the UN's resolution's failure and U.S. inaction might encourage the Assad government to intensify its violent crackdown on anti-government protesters, as evident from increased attacks in areas in protest against the Assad regime.

Obama is in a serious quandary. The Syrian army has continued to launch mortar and rocket attacks in the city of Homs, Syria's third-largest city, and the leading focus of unrest in the 11-month uprising against President Bashar al-Assad's rule. On the record Obama has openly stated that "Assad has no right to lead Syria, and has lost all legitimacy with his people and the international community." But in the eyes of the world he gives the locution of being selecting favorite as well as ignoring the same democratic principles he outlined for supporting a no-fly zone in Libya. Also, and more troubling, is his assertion that not every situation allows for the type of military action taken in Libya when his global middle –east policy purports otherwise.

Obama's actions are also affiliated with election year politics, since it may be seen that taking military options off the table is a political ploy to demonstrate his conviction to his campaigning on reducing US military intervention around the globe prior to election. Whatever the case, the US needs define their purpose and outcome in Syria as it pertains to the entire region. Thus the administrations proclamation that outside military involvement in Syria by the U.S. as being more difficult and risky than the mission in Libya appears disingenuous, especially to those nations in the Middle East whom we claim we desire to see democratic change.

The president in my estimation should not be dragged into another military exercise, in particular give his campaign promises of 2008 and his seemingly anxiousness to do all in his power to show how grand of a friend he is too the state of Israel. Truth is told this is nothing new to Syria. In February 1982, when Reagan was in the Whitehouse former Syrian President Hafez al-Assad initiated a brutal crackdown in the western Syrian city of Hama in order to quell an emergent uprising and a Sunni rebellion. The assault lasted for three weeks and Hama was effectively demolished. With the number of casualties estimated to be between 20,000 and 40,000 civilians, including women and children.

The Hama Massacre was the bloodiest event in Syrian history. President Hafez al-Assad was the father of the current president Bashar al-Assad. It should be remembered (and I hope President Obama does) that it occurred during a period during the aftermath of Israel's attack on Syrian forces in Lebanon in 1982. The administration of Ronald Reagan had to choose to support one of the two nations and landed on the side of Syria.

For the GOP to forget this history is strange. Maybe because it was a time when Donald Rumsfeld met with Saddam, to speak about regional issues of mutual interest, mainly their shared enmity toward Iran and Syria. No one asked Reagan to intervene in Syria in 1982, but everyone is asking

Obama to do so. My query is, what makes 2012 any different than 1982? A question no pundit or Republican will ever ask.

21

Undoubtedly the Obama Administration inherited a complete mess from the prior administration covering both the economy and foreign policy. And true to form, he in many respects has continued the aforesaid policies of the former president from the bail out of the Auto industry, TARP, extending the Bush tax cuts and even Bush's neoconservative foreign policy undertakings. In the classic sense, a large assemblage would propose that Obama's foreign policy strategy is diametrically opposite to the neoconservative hawks of the prior administration. Maybe, but in the verity of evidence suggest that the present administration has only morphed neoconservative dogma into neoliberal dogma.

This case can be made singularly by presenting the current Obama administration policies regarding Iran, Israel, Libya, and even tertiary nations like Nigeria, Somalia and the Congo. IT IS NOT FAR FETCHED TO draw the aforementioned parallel within a historical context. As a nation the foreign policy approach of the Obama administration to be fair, remains in the tradition of the fallacy of the first crusades which resulted in the capture of Jerusalem from the Seljuk Turks in 1099. This remains to be the premise of what we see between the West (U.S. and Europe) and the East (Arabs, Persians and Asians).

What do I mean you may ask? Well today as then, the U.S. represents the crusader state – meaning that our goals through foreign policy are to promote a universal culture of values "that must be spread throughout the world in the righteous cause of peace." This is the basic tenant of Wilsonian idealism the way I have understood political history and put in action by both Obama and Bush. Neoconservative appears to be conservative yet support and favor big government, interventionism, and hostility to religion in politics and government.

Neoconservatives played a small role in the Ronald Reagan Administration, but came out the closet during the George W. Bush Administration after 2001. In comparison, the same can be said of Obama whose primary foreign policy goal demonstrates zeal to expand world peace and preserve American exceptionalism at any cost.

As I recall, Obama campaigned against President Bush's policies, yet he continues most of these policies today. Like Bush, he has increased funding for U.S. Special Operations Command (SOCOM) and has quadrupled overseas deployments. In Somalia for example, the Obama administration "has put in place policies to limit food aid to the region, using food as a weapon of war and killing hundreds of civilians weekly via its use of U.S. drone strikes. Recently he has sent U.S. troops to oil rich Uganda (Uganda has yet to produce a single barrel of oil) to intervene militarily to help Uganda fight the rebels of the LRA who are currently in the Central African Republic. Recently, more information has surfaced asserting that the U.S. Army has been making "preparations for possible direct military intervention in Nigeria."

All I am saying is that the manner in which many pundits attacked neoconservative foreign policy was appropriate and the same amount of scrutiny needs to be directed at this new neoliberal foreign policy of Obama. The only difference between the two is not idealism but rather methodological. Bush proffered a less technological approach than Obama currently employs.

Although the present administration is providing the appearance of getting of Iraq and Afghanistan, Obama continues to stay the of Bush neoconservative policy in the Middle East pushing out longtime rulers, as was the case in Libya and as he is attempting to do in Syria. Albeit his first act as president was signing an executive order to close the facility holding terrorist detainees at Guantanamo Bay within a year, he still maintains the policy of the former administration as well as has continued a version of the Bush practice of renditions. I wonder how essential it was to hold and water boarded Khalid Sheikh Mohammed in a secret prison in Eastern Europe to help get info to identify Osama bin Laden's couriers?

Also, Obama in concert with Eric Holder continue the practice of indefinite detentions and continue to trample the civil liberties of US citizens just as Bush did with the Patriot Act and the FBI's ability to obtain certain phone records without warrants. The Obama's Justice Department has given legal authority for the continuation of these policies.

Now I did not get a chance to speak on the example of Ira and Israel, but I will and soon, just not here. The only point I wanted to try and make that the neoconservative philosophy many conservatives applaud today has not been removed from the current Whitehouse. In fact it has changed and mutated into a more vile policy perspective, that has taken us even further back to the times of the crusades, one which says to the world it is our way or the high way. My only concern is that other nations don't forget the pangs of neocolonial practices they see make nations like the U.S. richer, while they barely have food to eat and water to drink.

22

Unlike some folks, I remember the day the people of Iran overthrew the Shah in 1979. Looking at our current contrived grievance with Iran, I wonder if the present administration does. Over the past year, due to the omnipotent pressure and power of the U.S. Zionist lobby, we have seen multiple military attacks on Iran nuclear facilities and even the kidnapping and assassination of leading Iranian academics and scientist. We have even seen pressure placed on democrats by this lobby, in particular the loss of the New York 9th district congressional seat vacated by Anthony Weiner to such an extent that the president sent bunker buster bombs to Israel to appease their supporters. In fact just this New Year, Obama signed into law sanctions against Iran oil exports. I guess it was designed to show America's Jewish lobby and Israel that Obama is hard on Iran.

I have been taking my time writing on this because I want to see how all the chips fall. Just last month Treasury Secretary Timothy F. Geithner attempted to get Chinese policy makers to join an American-led campaign to reduce oil exports from Iran because of its nuclear program. However like Russia, they have rejected to participate in the U.S./European sanctions or the oil embargo directed toward the Persian nation. This will be problematic since it is the Treasury Departments responsibility to enforce sanction laws since the new legislation would prevent access by nations who do not support sanctions on Iran to the American financial system. Although loop holes in the law allow for selected exemptions, in all honestly, I do not think that the president, just as presidents past, is ready for what may exist on the horizon in an election year or to our economy. The Chinese trade surplus with the United States widened even more to 24.2 percent to $17.4 billion this past December.

China exports $1.5 trillion of its production and ships 20% of its exports to the U.S., which created a $252 billion trade deficit in 2010.Not to mention that as of last year China owned $1.16 trillion in U.S. debt in the form of Treasury bills, notes and bonds - 26% of the total of $4.5 trillion held by the public. For all practical terms this makes China America's largest banker, giving it leverage over the U.S. as evident when China threatens to sell part of its holdings whenever the U.S. pressures it to raise the value of the yuan. It is no wonder that the U.S. trade deficit with China in 2010 was 27 times larger than it was back in 1990.

Another concern is that some fear Russia fears Israel is pushing America to war on Iran "which could retaliate by blocking" Persian Gulf oil shipments. It is clear that Russia will do what it perceives as necessary to protect its strategically important Tartus, Syria base, its only Mediterranean one (there is as we speak a Russian aircraft carrier battle group is positioned nearby). Then we have 15,000 combat troops in Kuwait, inclusive of two Army infantry brigades and a helicopter unit along with two aircraft carrier battle groups remains in the region – so the President has to be careful from a geopolitical purview.

As it stands, the Obama policy is another political divertissement of imperious old men who have never been to war and like to say they have a right to prevent other nations from self determination, especially when it comes to developing nuclear power. Even it is in the form of weapons, history shows that the only folk who have used nuclear weapons have been the United States. So important is this that we will assist in the assignation of scientist – an act that if implemented by the Taliban or Iranians we would call terroristic. Now we have even indicated to them that any effort to control their own geopolitical borders via the Strait of Hormuz would evoke a swift response from the U.S. military. Again strange since we say one reason we are hard on Iran is because they are a vehicle for state sponsored terrorism.

To keep Israel happy Obama will likely find some excuse to save face, and maybe even attack Iran. As we speak, he is trying to gain support from Middle East allies in preparation for an impending US-Iranian confrontation. This is hard to understand for two reasons. First, we just got out of Iraq and are trying to get out of Afghanistan, why do we want another war so soon with a country of 75 million in which historically, sanctions have never worked. Moreover we as a nation cannot distance our self from targeted assassinations and other subversion in Iran.

He may as well give up on any support from China and when they and Russia do not go along, he will have do-do on his face because he will be powerless to do anything against them: Russia could damage our economy by artificially raising the price of crude oil and China by stop purchasing our debt and/or selling U.S. papers in bulk causing more devaluation of the dollar. I hope the Obama administration thinks this out, for every indication suggest that Washington, Israel and NATO allies cannot wait to bump heads with Iran and Syria. This even when the fact remains that no evidence whatever suggests an Iranian nuclear weapons program, according to the latest March 2011 US intelligence assessment.

Why is the White House plotting against Tehran when the living standards of the American working class continue to fall? According to Reuters, 23.7 million American workers are either unemployed or underemployed right now. I can figure out why spending billions on another military effort (war) is more important than spending that money here at home where it is needed.

What we do know is that Israel is believed to be the only nuclear-armed state in the Middle East and that although Iran states it has missiles capable of reaching Israel, it is questionable if could hit long-range targets accurately. Sure two years ago Iran said it would build 10 new uranium enrichment sites, the only thing the Obama Administration really has to hang its hat on is Israeli Prime Minister Benjamin Netanyahu desire for harsh action against the nation – not for nuclear weapons but rather for its civilian nuclear program, saying such technological advances serve as a threat to the entire world.

I am dumfounded that countries without oil, like France and Italy via French President Nicolas Sarkozy and Italian Foreign Minister Franco Frattini are demanding "immediate" actions against the Iranian government when any preemptive strike or military campaign against Iran will become a large weight on the global economy. Some have speculated that the price of oil may grow to $300 per barrel if military strikes against Iranian nuclear facilities occur. State Department spokesman Joseph Cirincione believes that a military operation against Iran will lead to a large-scale war and will only encourage Iran to develop nuclear weapons.

Thus any Israeli strikes against Iran will send shock waves across the region. Global markets fluctuate just on reports involving Iran. He cannot allow Israel to persuade the U.S. and Britain to start a war against Iran in order to prevent it from producing nuclear weapons because if oil prices increase in multiples, the most vulnerable economies (U.S. and Europe) will just suffer greatly. The same is true if the U.S. continues to impose more sanctions on Iran and Obama cannot afford such with gas prices at home rising more and more each day. As I write, oil hovers above $106 as Iran tensions mount meaning any conflict could lead to global crude supply disruptions. The announcement that Iran will stop selling oil to

Britain and France in retaliation for a planned European oil embargo this summer shows they aren't playing.

The fact is that, no evidence whatever suggests an Iranian nuclear weapons program, according to the latest March 2011 U.S. intelligence assessment. Ross knows it and so do some political and media heads, yet they suppress truth and promote confrontation and war. But the real outcome will be that a "Stronger-than-expected demand against limited inventory and scarce excess production capacity leaves the market extremely vulnerable to price spikes in the near-to-medium term," Goldman Sachs said in a report. "It is important to emphasize that a spike in oil prices would most likely inflict damage on the economic recovery."

Targeting Iran's nuclear program is a red herring and the real aim of the west is regime change and controlling strategic geopolitical regional resources. Israel doesn't have the best interest of the U.S. populous in mind and really don't care about us at all. They are hypocrites saying the desire a two state solution when never has been the case even since the Oslo accords. I mean how can you want a Jewish state without wanting an Islamic state? Not to mention, the arguments being made by Iran and their nuclear ambitions are similar as those presented by Israel pertain to the nuclear reactor at Dimona. As indicated earlier, Israel is in fact a nuclear power - the only nuclear power in the world that insists on behaving as if it were not one. They don't let UN inspectors in so how can they ask us to do their dirty work? Again, Obama and any future president need to see through this and get away from standing buy Israel at all cost. Would you stand by your friend if he was an admitted rapist or murderer? If we don't, we will find out who the real rogue state is and dragged down in what may turn out to be world war III.

23

"As President of the united States, I don't bluff." These were the words of President Obama, sounding as bellicose as the neocons of the prior administration and prior. I guess to take a lyric from a song from Sesame Street and replacing lulu with Be Be, "Be Be's back in town. Not to mention I'm sure it was to impress Mr. Netanyahu, Israel and the AIPAC Zionist lobbyist who vote he will definitely need for a second term.

The statement from my perspective was disappointing and demonstrates the president, as Bush, do not understand history nor evince the capacity to learn from it as if re-election is the paramount of all things. As it stands we have sanctions already in place against Iran and an oil embargo, why do we need to purport military action as our only form of redress? Who are we to ask another nation on behalf of Israel to not pursue nuclear ambitions? Israel has nuclear weapons and we as a nation are the only one to us them on another nations, thus it seems logical that one would expect Israel to use them before Iran or even the United States.

Israel is not and never has been honest in its announcement it affirms the necessity of Palestinian self-determination. Even at the end of the Reagan years when the PLO accepted UN resolutions 242 and 338 – recognizing Israel's right to exist within the 1967 borders. But still, Israel continues on its unilateral imperialistic religious intolerance and militaristic attacks against the good faith of Palestine and the diplomatic process.

The present administration, the way I see it may get the nation in a quandary if it continues to play "Charles Atlas" for it is not Israel who is having sand kicked in its face. They continue to build settlements and close Palestinian schools in the name of self-preservation and Zionism before truthful dialogue. All U.S. presidents in the recent decades have confronted this. Just review the relationship between Yitzhak Shamir and George Bush – it was Bush who pointed out in concert with James Baker the obstacle with expansion and new settlements in the occupied terror to peace.

The Palestinians only had about 20 percent of their homeland left after 1948 and live in less area given the settlements are connected by a maze of roadblocks and military checkpoints. For more than forty years Israel has ruled the West Bank in such a manner that has created a system of Zionistic apartheid. In 2008, they waged war against the Palestinian people again, from the way I see it, to shift attention from them dealing with the real issue. Although not simple, the fact remains that Israel interest and U.S. interest do not intersect let alone coincide. They ignore the reality of any solution that will require a Palestinian state and capital in East Jerusalem with folks who meanwhile take over the West bank giving praise to the beliefs of a psychopathic killer Baruch Goldstein.

Then here at home, if it's not the ADL it is AIPAC who would rather take the position of Be Be Netanyahu than a

65

sitting President of the United States of America. This is treason to me and maybe they should replace the "A" with an "I" and go to Israel. Last I looked they were not fighting two wars or shoulder to shoulder with U.S. service personnel in Iraq or Afghanistan.

Obama should forget even trying to convince this group of non-Americans and Israel of anything. Their interest as I have stated are not U.S. interest. Moreover the stuff we do to try and show them support are not doing any good for America. Even our Joints Chief of Staff has gone on record as saying the manner in which the state of Israel deals with Palestinians motivates the Muslim world to ferment anti-U.S. sentiment.

Obama, you need to be hard on Israel. We're not their sugar daddy. We say we have their back regardless but as an African American man, I know guilt by association. I know that I am not going to jail for a rapist or a murderer even if my friend. We need to take the same position. We need to tell them not to start a war straight up or hit them with sanctions, cut off all streams of our funding to them and better yet, tell them no more tanks or jets. We cannot trust Israel as history has demonstrated inordinate times.

If Israel goes ahead with airstrikes, Iran will hit us also (another reason supporting their position is not in U.S. interest). And If I were the President, no secret the U.S. would come before them and if they did send jets to strike Iran, I would shoot them down via a no fly zone.

A lot of U.S. don't read and would not remember how they tried to bait us into a war before. In 1967, the USS Liberty was attacked by unmarked Israeli jets and ships and resulted in the deaths of more than 30 U.S. service men, but this was covered up by Lyndon B. Johnson. I would not be surprised if they tried to do the same again and blame Iran.

Please Mr. President, do not fall into the trap of doing Israel's dirty work for them. In the end, it will be our economy and the blood of our young men and women who pay for their insolence. Military spending is already draining our economy and fighting for a Jewish state, when we in policy deplore Islamic states, is undemocratic in principal if it ignores the Christians and Muslims who occupy that same nation state also.

24

A decade later and we are still in Afghanistan. Those on the campaign trail for the GOP nomination are pontificating out the sides of their necks, John McCain is inveighing nonsense and the Obama administration is taking hits left and right – and rightly so. I have expressed my view on the U.S. occupation of the central Asian nation eve prior to Obama, but clearly to no avail. I regrettably do not have the ears of the president or media pundits. And God knows I would love to hear urban radio adduce such a discussion with clarity. However, it seems that discussions on the photographs of Whitney Houston in her coffin, her nineteen year old daughter and wondering whether or not Chris Brown and Rihanna will get back together are more important conversations to have in our communities. Not to mention any topic that panders to the absolute support and defense of President Obama regardless of the cost or reality.

First I need to address the assassination recently carried out by a U.S. solider (Robert Bales) in the heart of the region. Since the event, I have only heard sentiments of justification of his behavior, namely that he must have been mentally ill. I agree. But what strikes me as bazaar was that no such acceptance of mental illness (which is obvious to me) was ever pronounced for Maj. Nidal Malik Hasan, the U.S. Army psychiatrist who allegedly opened fire inside Fort Hood in Texas killing thirteen people and wounding 30 people. Any who.

To properly understand our central Asian foreign policy, a brief history of our approach to foreign policy philosophy is in order. After World War II, the significance of American exceptionalism supported and justified our interventionist policies. Basically, that as the "cosmic policeman", righteousness of our nationalism evinced the position that only the U.S. was the last best hope of mankind and the world. This was code for American aspirations of hegemony over much of the world and defined overtly that democratic globalism rather than the national interest of the United States were the central issues at heart when considering the utility of military intervention. As if our self-proclaimed moral righteousness was eugenically paramount over pragmatism.

Although the Cold War mentality was supposedly over, it continued to exist and it legacy revamped, via a conservative movement that pursued no strategic alternatives in our foreign other than military action. That leads us to present day Iraq and Afghanistan. First, we fail to recognize our approach to borders versus the people is setting us for failure. Until we deal with such as a Pashtun issue, we will continue to run around like a chicken with its head cut off. The region is occupied by what history would call the Scythians or the Saka, those folks who live on the land from the Black sea to China. This is where most of our concern is presently and our presence is cloaked under the guise of wanting a stable democratic government fin the region albeit facts assert that the characteristics required for the formulation of such governments are not existent in Afghanistan or Iraq.

This however has not stopped Bush or Obama for attempting to produce such an outcome. Even Bill Clinton, who supposedly was a progressive, had the same approach to foreign policy in Central Asia. All three have never provided any well defined objectives other than perpetual peace through the dream of a universal democratic order on the American model. This desire to see American political structure manifest in other regions is a consequence of our historical imperialistic and colonial roots and is no different under Obama as it was Bush. Look at Yemen for example. It is really just another open ended war designed to make us look good and feel good. But all it accomplishes is to add more debt and more ant-American sentiment in the region. Before this there was Iraq, a nation of only 24 million that was destroyed by U.S. military power with a 12-year U.S.-led economic embargo prior to the war and daily bombing which our Air Force destroyed most of Iraq's water purification plants and sewage systems, resulting in the deaths of more than 500,000 children from water-borne disease and lack of medicines alone. And all to protect the people and bring about peace through democracy. One thing we were able to accomplish was to increase the presence of Shia death squads that inflicted untold violent acts on Sunnis. Paul Wolfowitz, said that invading Iraq would cost a mere $40 billion and would be paid for by taking over its oil.

Post-Saddam Iraq will not be a pro-Western model of democratic stability. In particularly under the autocratic rule of Prime Minister Nouri al-Maliki, It will be a quasi-democratic state with a strong pro-Iranian orientation. Likewise in Pakistan, we will be left with a corrupt and ineffectual government run by President Hamid Karzai where the Taliban remains at full strength and growing. Was this what was our desire for producing a democracy under of the US model in a pursuit for universal peace?

I can't answer this, but I will assume the answer is no or else we would have not entered Libya. I mean, it too was based on humanitarian principles, to defend the civilian population based on the "responsibility to protect" doctrine that was used to justify Libya. It is strange since it is used selectively – not for Syria or the Sudan. Especially given that such an argument is more valid for Syria and the Sudan than it did in the case of Libya. Assad's and Umar Hassan Ahmad al-Bashir's militaries have killed way more people compared to just a few hundred deaths at the time of NATO's intervention against Gaddafi.

Fact is that just as the neoconservatives in the Bush administration, Obama is on a similar crusade to transform the Middle East. Both the Bush and Obama administrations have hidden the cost of our current Central Asian interventions from the American people by refusing to pay for it through taxes. Both continue the post-cold war legacy of the quest for universal democratic order based on the American democratic model and the desire to transform the Middle East and central Asia. The question is how are American interest defined in these military interventions outside of emotional terms? It is as if we have not received the memo.

Remember it was Hillary Clinton's State Department who suggested that Egypt appeared stable and opposition forces would not topple Hosni Mubarak's dictatorship. WRONG, and what we do know after elections is that a democratic Egyptian government won't be pro-U.S.

This is the definition of O-bushian nationalism. It means we spend trillions of dollars and the lives of thousands for the purposes of accomplishing nothing but establishing and entrenched hatred for America across the Muslim world with nations being more dangerous than when our troops first arrived. And all for merely not wanting to show weakness politically, for wanting to develop a stable democratic government without the request of the occupied nation with merely a threat on our emotions called terror and no U.S. interest involved.

25

First I want to give a shout out to all the African Americans out on the front line protesting against the horrible atrocities in the Sudan, especially those who have written diligently and criticized the president for his lack of attention toward that war torn nation. Not to pat myself on the back for writing about Obama and his lack of attention toward Africa, not to mention its descendents who helped him get in office, I have pressed the issue vehemently but only have received comments suggesting I stop "finding" stuff to complain about regarding our current commander in chief by his coterie of folk who protect him simple because of the color of his skin.

Last month, it took a wealthy White man to bring attention to what was occurring in Sudan. I was glad of the attention but was hurt at the same time that no one that looked like me was on the front row of this issue. I'm sure there will be many now, since the uncle tom gene that many of us possess is not a recessive gene and always stands out when master does something to say it's ok for us to follow masters lead.

This week, Sudan on Tuesday carried out new airstrikes inside South Sudan in around the village of Tashwin. This after Khartoum vowed that it would use "all means" against a three-pronged attack it said South Sudanese forces had launched against South Kordofan state, including its key oil-producing region of Heglig. These are a continuation of skirmishes that happened last month along the undemarcated and disputed frontier in the Heglig area, with each side blaming the other for starting the fighting.

The last time I heard the president even speak of the problems in Sudan was June of 2011. He was at the United Nations as his top envoy prepared to travel to the region to address the political and military crisis concerning the peaceful division of Sudan into two states. It was right after he had met with his top Sudan envoy, Princeton Lyman as representatives from northern and southern Sudan continued talks in Addis Ababa, Ethiopia. All he did was talk and give some warning and photo ops.

It is clear the focus and interest for the present administration is Syria for they turn a blind eye toward Sudan and Africa in general. I am certain that they are aware that Khartoum fought one of Africa's bloodiest and longest civil wars against the south - a 22-year conflict, which began in 1983 and left more than 2 million people dead.

This is what is so troubling, the visible inconsistency of Obama's foreign policy. He says nothing for example about Omar Al- Bashir, the dictator of Sudan and one of the worst mass murderers of our time who has committed genocide for longer than any political leader living currently. Obama is either hiding or intentionally avoiding this. On the one hand, it is easy for him to state that Hosni Mubarak , Muammar Qaddafi and Syria's Bashar al-Assad must go but not Al-Bashir, the tyrant right next door to a ruler who was way less dangerous to his people comparatively speaking and much less monstrous - Qaddafi. When reality in the form of displacement, deaths and rapes supports that chasing Qaddafi and not Al-Bashir is like "going after Mussolini instead of Hitler. "

Last March I wrote, "not to beat a dead horse, but this Libya example is almost comical. The reasons proffered for intervention are even more fanatical, when we look at and ex-

73

amine the desire to protect the innocent. Maybe the innocent dwellers of lands endeared with oil reserves, but not solely the innocent. By that logic, worthy locations would have our attention. The Sudan where millions are having been displaced and tens of thousands butchered. The Ivory Coast, where more than 500,000 have been displaced and a civil war looms".

Just last October, the President issued a series of waivers for the Child Soldiers Protection Act (a 2008 law that is meant to stop the United States from giving military aid to countries that recruit soldiers under the age of 15 and use them to fight wars) for Yemen, South Sudan, Chad, and the Democratic Republic of the Congo. Not forgetting that as of 2010 the allocation of U.S. foreign aid from USAID to Sudan was in excess of $420 million. A continuance in the pattern of continuous involvement with foreign aid to Sudan for many years in which more than $250 million was given to the nation between 1977–1981.

But for the Obama administration, the fledgling democratic movement of the Sudan must be defended and preserved even at the cost of millions lives of innocent and defenseless civilians—children, women, and men. When he was a senator, in 2007 and 2008, Obama, was extremely critical of George W. Bush's administration for engaging with Khartoum. Obama even advocated for a no-fly zone for Darfur. Even his current U.N. ambassador, Susan Rice advocated military intervention with personnel on the ground. Also in 2008, then candidate Obama joined in a statement in which he demanded "that the genocide and violence in Darfur be brought to an end and that he would "pursue these goals with unstinting resolve." Not to mention a year later it was Mr. Obama, in a statement released by the White House who said "As the United States and our international partners meet our responsibility to act; the government of Sudan must meet its responsibilities to take concrete steps in a new direction."

The Whitehouse lacks an official policy toward the Sudan and to this date has not keeping his campaign promises, although Obama once said, "Sudan is a priority for this Administration" and "There must be real pressure placed on the Sudanese government." Barack Obama says that the US will apply more pressure on Sudan but his administration has caved to a flawed election. I guess assuming that such is better than no election at all. The fact is that the present administration ignorance and inaction most likely end in a new civil war. The last north-south civil war in Sudan ended with a fragile peace in 2005, after some two million deaths.

What is our administration's foreign policy when it comes to dictators, tyrants, Africa and democracy? Obama claims he went to war in Libya because NATO was afraid of the threat of government genocide, while we see such real time in the Sudan. Now the Administration is turning its attention and rhetoric towards Syria; which I am certain is for the benefit of Israel.

I just want the president to come correct and say openly that he has no interest in addressing what is going on in Africa with the Sudan. That he and his administration has a lack of interest in the slaughters of Africans whenever it involve people with darker skin. The numbers reported that I have seen pertaining to Sudan is greater than those in Libya or Syria, yet the White House seems not to notice. Even in the dictionary, Sudan would come before Syria.

26

Okay, I didn't want to but I feel as if it is my duty. Reason waits for no one to present timely analysis in a world in which billions of dollars are spent to wage war on emotions such as terrorism in places like Somalia alone, when poverty continues to expand and metastasize by leaps and bounds her at home. Nor could I wait for common televised media outlets to present breaking news, seeing they are two days behind print media, which is two days behind the internet. Not to mention it is obvious the televised media's goal is identical to the rule of oppression, based on the incessant rash of treatments inundated with coverage of George Zimmerman, the secret service and any one of several reality shows purporting to display talent, it is unthinkable that the presentation of actual news content is important or possible.

What am I speaking of, deals with China and the Philippines and a possible new war on the horizon between the U.S. and China. I have been leery of this possibility for sometimes ever since President Obama decided to ramp up U.S. alliances and bases across Asia and in the Pacific. The president basically asserted that the U.S. start to focus on Asian security risks including China and North Korea, which have over the past decade taken a back seat to Iraq and Afghanistan. From this perspective, the United States will maintain large bases in Japan and South Korea and deploy U.S. Marines, navy ships and aircraft to Australia's Northern Territory. It also deals with, if necessary, to be in a position to counter possible efforts by China and Iran to block U.S. capabilities in areas like the South China Sea and the Strait of Hormuz. In essence, this was Obama's presentation at a special trip to the Pentagon this past January. It was basically his post-Iraq, post-Afghanistan defense strategy.

During his Asian tour, Obama signaled the opening of a military base in Darwin and possibly one in the Philippines. Although we have solid ballistic missile defense co-operation with Japan is well advanced, this has more to do with North Korea and China.

Now things are increasingly becoming more on edge. Just this week the Philippines announced it would be seeking additional U.S. military help during top-level talks next week, as it becomes more involved with China over a territorial dispute. Calling on a treaty signed in 1951, Philippines Foreign Secretary Albert del Rosario indicated the desire for United States to help it achieve a "credible" defense system. The treaty calls on both sides to come to each other's aid in times of external attacks. Currently the island nation is in disagreement with Beijing over rival claims to the West Philippines Sea (South China Sea). China claims all of the West Philippine Sea as a historic part of its territory, even waters close to the coasts of the Philippines.

Over the past few weeks, armed vessels from the Philippines and China have faced off at the Scarborough Shoal.

The consequences for the US if this occurs would be another undeclared war we would be dragged into; especially if Manila gets its way and obtains the coast guard vessel and F-16 fighter jets it recently requested. The Philippines is leading a push within the 10-member Association of South-East Asian Nations (ASEAN) to take a united stand over regional maritime disputes, including the Spratly Islands, an archipelago in one of the world's busiest stretches of water.

Then there are other geopolitical concerns involved. The Philippines' Malampaya and Camago fields are estimated to hold 4.4 trillion cubic feet of natural gas and are in waters currently claimed by China. To top it off, as you read this, the U.S. and the Philippines are engaged in annual joint military exercises that have involved 4,500 U.S. soldiers and 2,500 from the Philippines.

Defense Secretary Leon Panetta announced these intentions a week before the start of April, which he said showed U.S. commitment to the strategically vital Asia-Pacific region. But such was in the work as early as last December when the Obama Administration signaled plans for the deployment of 2,500 Marines to Darwin, Australia. Darwin is also an intriguing choice since it is part of a growing energy hub where companies including Royal Dutch Shell Plc (RDSA) are planning to spend more than a $150 billion ($156 billion) to develop offshore natural gas fields.

Given all of the aforementioned, it may not be farfetched to suggest a possible future military conflict with China. Already the Chinese state media has advanced that

President Barack Obama is doing all of this to distract from U.S. economic woes, which is logical seeing that the Pentagon is placing more troops in the region than at any time since World War II, with military outpost surrounding all of China's eastern border (the U.S. is sending 4,700 Marines to Guam, creating the largest deployment of troops to the Pacific since World War II). Meanwhile, China is rapidly expanding its naval power and increasing its presence in the South China Sea.

Moreover, an ironic observation is that China is also increasing its naval power and their new the refurbished Soviet aircraft carrier Varyag is almost fully operational. In concert with a new seaport being built by the Philippine government in the Spratly islands, in which such would be the first step in creating a mini-naval base for U.S. and Philippine troops, we could see more action sooner than later; in particular with Vietnam and the Philippines beginning to develop stronger military ties with the US.

Last year Chinese ships confronted a Philippine oil-exploration ship as well as cut a Vietnamese oil-exploration vessel's survey cable. In response, Vietnam later conducted a live-fire naval drill in the area. China has also expressed its concerns over statements made by the U.S. chief of naval operations, Admiral Jonathan Greenert, that China's rising capability could limit U.S. access to the South China Sea and that Washington would continue its efforts to ensure freedom of navigation there. The comments were interpreted by some observers as confirming that the U.S. has sided with the ASEAN claimants.

The installation in the Spratly islands could also be used as a jumping-off point for counterterrorism operations in the Palawan region of the southern Philippines. The area is home to the Abu Sayyaf, an Islamic terror groups with ties to al Qaeda. Some early reports from France suggest the new facility on Pagasa Island will be the new home for thousands of U.S. Marines scheduled to leave Okinawa within the next two years.

All of this sounds similar, a military buildup in the name of counter acting emotion in the name of terrorism; making enemies we don't need, with a nation that hold the largest portion of U.S. debt, 68 cents for every dollar or about $10 trillion; and a currency battle that is still in the frying pan, all makes sense to me – our next war will probably be in the South Pacific.

27

In *Areopagitica*, John Milton wrote: "*Let truth and falsehood grapple: whoever knew truth, put to the worse, in a free and open encounter?*"

He wrote this in 1644 as an appeal to the English Parliament to end a political order that attempted to bring all publishing under control by official government censors (authors would submit their work for approval prior to having it published). It is a terse yet polemical parallel to the Areopagiticus of Isocrates and the story of the apostle Paul in Athens from Acts 17: 18-34. It pertained to the "degradation of the judges of the Court of the Areopagus, the highest court in Greece". However, one can also apply this to political tyranny axiologically as well, in particular when it concerns facts as a function of political action and mandate.

Over the past few years, the Obama administration has increased rather aggressively its foot print, militarily speaking, in Africa. Under the guise of fighting for the righteous neoliberalim to defeat tyranny and kleptocratic rule in the name of democracy, the Obama administration has boldly implemented a path in Africa similar to those seen in past history, especially that of King Leopold II (1835-1909).

In 1876, Belgium's King Leopold II held a conference in Brussels in which he asserted that Western nations should establish an international benevolent committee for the propagation of civilization among the peoples of Central Africa (the Congo region). Between the years of 1878 to 1884, it resulted in an eventual Belgian sovereignty, in the Congo Basin. His primary objective was to exploit the lucrative ivory and rubber market in Central Africa. After proclaiming sovereign Belgium state rights, and via three successive decrees, Leopold asserted rights of proprietorship over all vacant lands throughout the Congo territory and reduced the rights of the Congolese in their land to native villages and farms. His goals were so colonialist and imperialistic that those who refused or failed to supply enough rubber often had their villages burned down, children murdered, and their hands cut off.

It is now 2012, and President Obama is seemingly on the same path. It started in Libya with a fake and non-extant humanitarian mission to protect the citizens of the oil-rich African nation. However it resulted in the merciless and brutal overthrow of a government and the death of a leader, Muammar Gaddafi who was making progress and vowed to create a 'United States of Africa' after his election as head of the African Union. Since last November, we have observed President Barack Obama send U.S. troops to Africa to help hunt down the leaders of the Lord's Resistance Army in and around Uganda. In his own words, Obama stated, "I believe that deploying these U.S. armed forces furthers U.S. national security interests and foreign policy and will be a significant contribution toward counter-LRA efforts in central Africa". Ironically is just as Libya, Uganda is sitting on tons of oil. Oil exploration began in Uganda's northwestern Lake Albert basin nearly a decade ago and according to estimates by the Energy Ministry, the African nation has over two billion barrels of oil. And as I wrote last October, billionaire George Soros is a member of its executive board and he just recently recommended the U.S. deploy a special advisory military team to Uganda.

Additionally, in the fall 2009, the Obama administration announced a security assistance package for Mali – valued at 4.5 to 5.0 million dollars – that included 37 Land Cruiser pickup trucks, communication equipment, replacement parts, clothing and other individual equipment and was intended to enhance Mali's ability to transport and communicate with internal security forces throughout the country and control its borders. Plus, his recently passed NDAA contained $75 million in U.S. aid aimed at fighting in Somalia and arming forces, particularly from Uganda and Burundi, as well as the armies of Djibouti, Kenya and Ethiopia.

Over the past few weeks, after the coup in the West African country of Mali, it has been uncovered that Capt. Amadou Haya Sanogo, who led a renegade military faction that deposed Mali's democratically elected president, has been in the United States several times to receive professional military education and training. Although official Obama administration doesn't support the overthrow of the formerly elected leader and that the U.S. Africa Command has suspended military cooperation with Mali, U.S. military personnel continue to deploy to Mali in part of a so-called Joint Planning Assistance Team.

I can go on with more, yet I digress. The goal is to point out, as Milton asserted, that when "truth and falsehood" do battle, truth always wins "in a free and open encounter". We know that he has sent military advisors which are still on the ground in Nigeria and have had them there since 2009. I find it ironic that our first African American President would be the one, as Leopold did, to establish a permanent U.S. military base in Africa, for the advancement of a long-range Anglo-American geopolitical agenda for Africa.

The query is does it serve our best interest? Is it for the benefit of Africa or is it to challenge China's economic interests in Africa? Or is it to reinvigorate the west past preoccupation with raping Africa for its resources for other plutocratic interest? In the past there were for human resources mainly for the utility of mining and slavery, today they are natural resources in the name of oil, gold, diamonds, nickel, palladium, copper, zinc, silver or others? We already have U.S.

special forces and other military personnel on the ground in five African nations and that's just on the record.

If my postulate is true and the aforementioned is even remotely plausible, then we should get ready for more famine, death, disease and all as the result of contrived wars in the name on benevolence as suggested by Leopold or national security as detailed by President Obama. Simple fact is that one cannot have either benevolence or security when the outcome is poverty, genocide and morbidity.

28

Maybe it is me but it strikes me as strange that first, all we hear about with respect to civil and human rights being violated pertains to Syria and there is no mention of Sudan, and two that for some reason the Obama Administration, the Congress and mainstream media has been extremely hush hush about Israel. Whether it involves the $1 billion for Israeli missile projects the U.S. House of Representatives allocated for the 2013 fiscal year for Israel's missile systems via the House Appropriations Defense Subcommittee appropriated USD 947 million for the Iron Dome, "David's Sling" and a long-range Arrow missile program; or how recent actions of the Zionist nations, in both statement and action are reminiscent of apartheid and the southern United States circa 1960s. The prior is in addition to the $5billion a year that Israel already receives in grants and doesn't have to pay back.

This is very disturbing to me in particular when our politicians want to jump around and turn up about being ready to protect human rights in Syria, yet seem to have money for Israel and not the millions of American citizens suffering at home. Not to forget all the time proclaiming we should stand for what is just around the world as the preeminent nation state in the world but say nothing when Jews call Africans nigger and beat them violently like the righteous citizens of Georgia, Alabama, and Mississippi did to African Americans. Susan Rice even has the audacity to get on her high horse suggesting action in Syria while never even mentioning the Sudan or what African immigrants are suffering under the rule of the world's only Zionist state.

In the predominately black neighborhood of Hatikva large groups of nationalist protesters who are vehemently open against African migrants have instigated a reign of terror similar to Nazi and KKK hate groups of past around the world. The Jewish protesters claim the Africans are responsible for a rise in crime, and were holding signs that read "this is not Africa" and "stop talking, start expelling". They even yelled "Blacks out!" and "send the Sudanese back to Sudan".

The mob set fires and smashed the windows of shops owned by Eritrean migrants, threw rocks at them and violently beat up Africans walking through the streets. According to one Nigerian witness, "a group of about 10 or 15 boys stopped one black kid cycling on his bike. They pulled him off and were punching and kicking him in his head. The police just stood and watched until it got really out of control." They even beat women carrying their infants and stopped buses to search for African passengers.

The United States gives more military aid to Israel than to any other country, although this is really not in the national interests of the United States or any net strategic advantage to the U.S. in sending weapons to Israel when compared to spending the same amount of money on improvements at home. Why is the question, because the state of Israel and Zionism is the antithesis of democracy? Factually speaking, Zionism is a racist political philosophy in the same vein as Nazism, and Apartheid. As a nation, the daily actions often consist of those we once saw in South Africa. These include millions of non-Jews who are under curfew and blockade, starving and brutalized, in the Middle East's only colonized state. This is not a wild exaggeration when we study the writings and speeches of racist Vladamir Jabotinsky, father of revisionist Zionism.

Zionism like racism espouses an independent and sovereign Jewish state, in a land where there is no Jewish majority and exists only insofar as it has been allowed to expel the people of Palestine from their homes, although it is against their basic human right guaranteed by Article 13 of the Universal Declaration of Human Rights. This means it is impossible for such to be a democratic principle when only one community and people benefit from such and not others. I can say this with ease being a logically thinking person since facts demonstrate that Zionism absolutely requires that Palestinians and even Africans, as non-Jews, be forced to leave in 1948 and never be allowed to return - blatant racism.

What these recent attacks on Africans show us is that all who are not Jewish in a Zionist state will be confronted with considerable discrimination. It is even more lucid and totally obvious that the force behind the policies of the present and all past Israeli governments in Israel and in the occupied lands was designed and implemented to assure the predominance of Jews over other racial-ethnic groups. For when a powerful nation like Israel that "kills hundreds of civilians from another ethnic group; confiscates their land; builds vast housing complexes on that land for the exclusive use of its own nationals" and does not offer equal protection to non Jews, that is not democracy but racist.

What happened then continues today, without any major media news coverage is racism at its worse. In particular when speakers at such events include prominent politicians, like Knesset ministers Miri Regev, Danny Danon, Yari Levin and Michael Ben-Ari. Ms. Regev during her address to the crowd even described African immigrants as a "cancer in our society". Danny Danon, a member of Benjamin Netanyahu's Likud party, wrote in a Facebook status later the same evening: "Israel is at war. An enemy state of infiltrators was established in Israel, and its capital is south Tel Aviv."

There are around 60,000 African asylum seekers in Israel, most from Eritrea and Sudan. Although she did not retract her statements, Ms. Regev stated "Israel should adopt the U.S. protocol of returning infiltrators to the border within 72 hours. Jews and Israelis are scared of living in their country" she said and although only non-Jews were the objects of violence Mr.

87

Danon desires to deport the city's African residents "to detention facilities and remove Africans from population centers".

Obama and Susan Rice cannot turn a blind eye to this as well as the average American citizen. From my perspective, I am unable to have disdain for what is going on in Syria without having the same bad taste for Israel and their treatment of Africans or the massive deaths occurring daily in the Sudan (more than Syria). Racism and xenophobia are huge problems in Israel society that we ignore as a nation. We should hold Israel's feet to the flame as we do other nations, making them abide by the 1951 UN Refugees convention since Israel is one of the signatory nations. If we do not, we will at least learn something: that in Israel if you are black, they call you nigger too and beat you like the KKK and white citizens councils did across the south in America.

29

I want to write a few paragraphs to present my understanding of the current Syrian quagmire. But in order to do this, it requires that I be in contradiction to the Obama Administration's position on that nation, a brief comprehension of history, and above all, objectivity.

The way I have evaluated the U.S. interest in Syria, it would purport what Israel desires toward Iran and nothing else is the focal point of this U.S. and NATO instigation against Assad. First, it is clearly evident that Palestinian's know that Israel will not grant them a state unless it is forced to do so. This position has shown itself in overt terms via the election to the Egyptian presidency of Muhammad Mursi of the Muslim

Brotherhood. Second, the economy more so than the protection of civilians or the desire for democratic transition is more essential for U.S. economic interest than political interest; how else are we to keep our money making defense industries alive unless we are in incessant battle with terrorism, regardless if it exist or not?

For the record, the Syria we know today did not exist until a treaty was signed, at the end of August, in 1920 after World War I. The signing occurred in Sevres, France, between the Ottoman Empire (Turkey) and the Allies. It is important to recall that this treaty destroyed the Ottoman Empire and Turkish sovereignty, but resulted in the sovereignty of Mesopotamia (Iraq), Palestine and Jordan. In the process, Palestine and Jordan were basically given to the British and Syria (including Lebanon), were given to the French. Turkey retained Anatolia but was to grant all of the aforementioned areas under the Treaty of Lausanne which was signed on 24th of July 1923.

However, since then the region has continued to show incessant signs of instability, namely because of the U.S. interest in maintaining the desires of Israel over the self determination of other nations. Now, the Obama administration has inherited this shaky instability and obviously feels that the progressive approach as presented via example before him by Woodrow Wilson and Teddy Roosevelt, and even Truman is the best way for the United States to go, even if that means developing proxy wars on the behalf of the interest of other nations (Israel) over the interest of the U.S.

In simple terms the U.S. and NATO are employing what they did in Libya and using it as a model to destabilize Syria, by hook or crook if needed. It may be hard for many to comprehend this if they lack a sufficient knowledge of the policies of Wilson and Truman, or worse, if they only believe and accept without query what is being fed to them by U.S. mainstream media. The obvious outcome based on actions by all parties involved to date, will be a bombing attack on Iran's nuclear and missile facilities, contingent upon the ousting of the current Syrian leadership, thus, using the resulting chaos of a failing Syrian state as a disguised attack on Iran. Given the history of Turkey after World War I, the U.S. will use them to serve as cover for deposing Assad and their subsequent attack on Iran – all which singularly benefit Israel.

Unbeknown to most, weapons from Saudi King Abdullah and Israel and possibly fed via the CIA are being sent to the rebels as I write. And I would not be surprised if the Saudi are not prepared with tanks and Special Forces to enter Jordan both to protect Jordan's King Abdullah against potential reprisals from Syria, Iran and even Iraq (yes Iraq) and attack Syria.

Obama has worked this out with Israel, knowing that Iran, Syria, and Iraq are mainly Shiite and the Saudi's are mostly Sunni. This will result in a Western-Arab-Turkish alliance military operation against Syria and eventually Iran. The problem is that Israel is still the target of most Arab states and that our present support for Islamist terrorists in Syria may proffer more risk than the present administration anticipates. We saw this before with Osama Bin Laden, who was cared for in the later stages of his kidney illness by the CIA's own doctors for his support in waging war against the Soviet Union in Afghanistan (who eventually turned on the U.S.) and Anwar al-Awlaki, also a CIA work horse who was even once invited to the Pentagon for dinner.

Although U.S. media has not informed the public of such, the reality is just as in Libya, Afghanistan, and Iraq; the Syrian people do not want any Western intervention in their country. Under the guise of "humanitarianism" the Obama administration has begun to wage an undeclared war on Iran in concert with Israel. Although the record indicates that talks between Iran and the UN Security saw the United States refuse to compromise when a deal was available whereby Iran would give up enriching uranium to 20% in exchange for an easing of sanctions and recognition of its right under the Nuclear Non-Proliferation Treaty to produce nuclear fuel for peaceful purposes. Instead, we accepted Israel's demand that Iran be forced, by means of further sanctions and military threats, to suspend all enrichment. That is strange when Israel and the U.S. have nuclear weapons.

I cannot place all of this at the feat of Obama, albeit his neocolonial aggressiveness has resulted in the deposition of more leaders of sovereign states than any presidents prior. Let's face it, after all the uproar with Libya, we hear nothing about the nation now. Although we know that the ones we called "freedom fighters" have turned out to be sectarian terrorists now carrying out a brutal campaign of nationwide torture, illegal imprisonments, and genocide across the nation.

Once all in Libya had free electricity – now they do not, and I will not mention how they are treating Black Africans. Entire towns have been wiped out with from ethnic and religious cleansing leaving the rest leaving the country for their lives. I will not mention Somalia and several other African nations.

Yes this is our Syrian foreign policy in a nutshell. It's not our policy and it isn't about Syria. It's Israel's policy and it's about Iran. In fact, according to U.S. Army General Wesley Clark, since the early 1990's he has been aware of a plan to overthrow the "old client regimes" of the Soviet Union. In the post-9/11 era, the same efforts were resurfaced to invade and overthrow the governments of seven specific nations, Iraq, Syria, Lebanon, Libya Somalia, Sudan, and Iran as told by General Clark himself during a presentation he made at the Commonwealth Club of California, October 3, 2007.

30

Obama should think twice about Iran. More and more each day it appears that the U.S. is inching its way closer to an armed conflict with Iran -- something I think will hurt the U.S. more than Israel in the long term. It is all because the big bully on the block, Israel, is purported to be "facing grave danger". This is mainly being promoted by Zionist from everywhere this side of the Pecos River. My question is why do we have to defend Israel, a nation with the largest army and only nuclear arsenal in that region?

We all are well aware of the fact that Israel is no friend of Iran, or of any other Islamic and predominantly Arab state in the region. Thus, Israel is the one making trouble yet they want the present administration to decide to launch a pre-emptive war in what are probably the world's most volatile environs.

If history is any guide, we should be very careful about deciding to attack Iran. Prior to WW 2 it was the Germans who convinced the "enlightened civilization" that it only wants to execute its rights. But one war led to another and country upon country was invaded including France, Belgium, the Netherlands and other countries. Now it is Israel, and they will only be happy when all of the other Arab nations are not just a threat, but nonexistent; for like Germany, their goal is not defensive but an aggressive offense to conquer the entirety of Middle East Asia.

True, it is hard to assess whether to "confront" or to "contain" Iran without examining more than 300 years of contemporary Iranian history, in concert with the history of conflict in the Middle East throughout modern times. Then we must decide and determine, if possible, what we are trying to prevent or contain them from doing; otherwise we will formulate policy, which has become customary, based on anger, fear, and hatred singularly. Even worse, one in which Israel must not be allowed to drive the world into chaos, just because it wants to. We need to protect AMERICA's interests, first, last, and always, and America's interests do not include shedding more blood for Israel or carrying their water for them. We've lost too many American lives already to satisfy Israel's demands over Iraq. But, apparently, we have learned nothing from Iraq, and Israel doesn't care as long as they get their way.

The only difference now is that the false flag of preventing a nation from self-determination in the form of developing nuclear capability is the issue. Albeit both the U.S. and Israel have such capabilities and past history reveals that the U.S. vowed that Pakistan or North Korea would never be allowed to possess nukes. Why should it be any different with Iran?

Factually, given our present quagmires in Iraq and Afghanistan and our bombing of our present alley Pakistan daily, a confrontation with Iran would also last for years and possibly crush America's economy – especially for the average American. Thus any form of military intervention at all in Iran means that the American taxpayer should be ready to pay $5 plus for a gallon of gas if a war breaks out in the Strait of Hormuz. We are already in a recession at best and depression at worse and hyperinflation is everywhere we look.

Next, we must try and anticipate what will happen as a function of if either side wins. After WW II, half of Europe ended up being given to the Soviets. Then due to our wasteful war effort in Iraq, in essence we have succeeded nearly half of this state to Iran. For both of these operations we as a nation have nothing really to show for it, except ending up in bed with the most treacherous leaders in modern times the likes of Mubarak, Pavlavi, House of Saud, Saddam Hussein, Khomeini, Assad and yes, the Likud.

The current administration still has Kool-Aid pumping through its veins. Sure, they went into Libya and are now selling wolf tickets about Syria; but the U.S. needs to think about these actions and the global political consequences. We need to stop demanding that Syrian President Bashar al-Assad step down and cease the threats because it shows hypocrisy when we decide and shout to the world who we think should step down from the position of a head of a state, in particular when we aren't prepared to remove that person. Then we talk about democracy when in fact to suggest the aforementioned is in contradiction of our own values.

Also, who cares if Israel is our strongest ally in the region, forget a clear and strong commitment to the security of Israel: the U.S. government should only have that strong of a commitment to the U.S. If they don't like how we do our thing then stop giving them loot. We should stick to our guns when we say that Netanyahu and Israel should use the 1967 borders and should be a basis for the negotiation of a Palestinian state. And for those who believe that Israel is our friend, they are not and only care about Israel. In the past, they have attacked one of our naval ships, killed our sailors, spied on us, and treated us like a vassal state.

I say let's us pack up the American-Israel Public Affairs Committee, the most powerful pro-Israel lobby in Washington, and send them to Israel and let them fight their own war. If they do, and if Israel attacks, the United States may get drawn into a war that could set the Middle East further aflame and no telling how bad global markets will get.

Iran is a country of 80 million people, compared with about 30 million in Afghanistan or Iraq. Its territory of 1.65 million square kilometers, including deserts and rugged mountains, gives it impressive strategic depth compared to Israel, which exists on 20,000 square kilometers. Even to attack Iran by air, Israel would have to strike Iran's four major nuclear sites. The most direct path to do so is across Jordan and Iraq. Will Jordan allow Israel to fly over? Then, Israeli pilots have to fly more than 1,600 kilometers refueling in the air, fighting off Iran's air defense, while attacking multiple underground sites at the same time.

Moreover, Iran is a major oil producer located right by the most critical petroleum and gas supply lines in the world, from the Strait of Hormuz in the south to the Caspian Sea in the north. I'm lost that military intervention is even being considered, because if it happens, it will introduce a whole new destabilizing reality into the Middle East.

And although the U.S. will try not to have a land war, we can't tell what will happen, or know the outcome. Will it be a war of attrition or an all-out invasion? We do know it will be long, money wasting. We cannot forget that in Europe in 1914, a small and unexpected event began the First World War. Obama really needs to think carefully about this. The sad reality is if America and our national security and safety were placed first – we would not attack Iran. However, he has learned from Bush, who has had the U.S. in Iraq for more than 10 years and resulted in a sustained U.S. military presence for 11 years in Afghanistan as we speak.

31

As I write, this, I already anticipate a backlash from the mass of Obama felatio administrators within the African American community, but I know all too well as Huxley wrote, "facts do not cease to exist because they are ignored and that one cannot argue with an idiot for they will beat you down with experience and win every time.

The situation which the U.S. finds itself in Syria was all our doing and 99.9 percent of the blame can be placed at the feet of the current Administration, President Barack Obama in particular. For it is President Obama's incoherent and fatuous policy in Libya based on the use of force when he wants to when U.S. national security is not even in jeopardy that got Ambassador Steven's killed.

It all started last year. First, President Obama ignored the constitution and decided, without Congressional approval, albeit he didn't agree with such when the same thing was done by former President George W. Bush just four years ago. In fact while being interviewed by the Boston Globe as a senator Obama said: "the president does not have the power under the constitution to unilaterally authorize a military attack in a situation that does not involve stopping an actual or imminent threat to the nation. History has shown us time and again...that military action is most successful when authorized and supported by the legislative branch."

The fact is that this same man singlehandedly committed the U.S. to war against Libya, ignoring that the U.S. had neither been attacked by nor was in danger from Libya and had no constitutional reason for any military intervention at all. I repeat, the president does not have power under the constitution to unilaterally authorize a military attack in a situation that does not involve stopping an actual or imminent threat to the nation.

But it was clear that being a constitutional scholar he was not concerned about this. In an address to the nation delivered from the National Defense University in March 2011, a day before the military effort against Gaddafi's forces, the president spoke of U.S. military action in Libya and indicated that NATO would be taking the lead from the U.S. adding that America's role in Libya would be to defend those under attack by Gaddafi's forces. This, he said, although the U.S. runs NATO, finances 22 percent of NATO's budget, and is the nation that gives all the marching orders. In essence Obama unilaterally decided to invade a sovereign nation as Bush did before him. Strangely enough, his assertion was that military action in Libya was in the vital interest of the U.S. This was his position albeit Defense Secretary Robert Gates noted that the events in Libya were not in the "vital national interest to the United States."

Despite Obama's incessant statements suggesting that the operation is only to protect civilians, the military intervention aid the rebel factions in their advance against the African leader. Although he will not admit to such, President Obama is an interventionist who on the one hand stated he had no desire for U.S. military intervention in Libya, noting that the U.S. will not use military invention, yet imposed a no-fly zone which in fact is "direct military intervention."

What the president called U.S. "humanitarian intervention" directed at a nonexistent U.S. aggressor undermined the concept of collective security, international law, and worst of all is arbitrary. Obama's Libyan policy was historically the same as his predecessor and allowed him, on behalf of America, to exploit weaknesses and divisions in the nations they interfere with all willy nilly.

His prose had continued to justify these actions. He said, "Some nations may be able to turn a blind eye to atrocities in other countries. The United States of America is different. And as president, I refused to wait for the images of slaughter and mass graves before taking action." But words and fancy slogans do not make up for the observation that he had never considered the ramifications of such actions. The question remains Mr. President if this was an issue of U.S. national security, did your actions in Libya make America safer?

Attacking Gaddafi got him lynched and one wonders if the administration ever asked or thought if this outcome would endear and make Libyans thankful for this? A nation which is already hated and which view America as constantly attacking Islam and taking their oil. Not to mention, was there any after thought that what had just occurred with the attack on the U.S.

mission, that killing or attacking Gaddafi without destroying his regime is just asking for increased terrorism against Americans? Or whether or not replacing him with insurgents who include other sponsors of terrorism, namely al Qaeda was really a good idea?

This is the backward neoliberal foreign policy logic that Obama uses and was adopted and modified based on Bush's neoconservative policy. We support dictatorships in Yemen, Bahrain and Saudi Arabia and say nothing, yet maintain a different standard for the same actions as it pertains to Libya and currently Syria.

Obama policy in Libya in concert with the senseless deaths of Libyan people is what created this opening for those who would love nothing more than to destroy America. The recent events give more substance to the position of China and Russia regarding Libya then and Syria which was: "if you try to impose anything on others, the result will be disastrous."

Obama's foreign policy, for a man who was awarded the Nobel Peace Prize, is the antithesis to the concept of state sovereignty, for it appears that state sovereignty is only problematic to the U.S. when it is applied to places like Libya or Syria. Notwithstanding nations who have had decades of general peace, which Obama policy has now replaced with war and violence and instability. The Obama Administration's foreign policy is typical of U.S. progressive presidents who take any self-selected event or issue as a reason to self-invite the U.S. to enter conflicts it has no reason to join, especially if national security is the standard (i.e. Woodrow Wilson, Teddy Roosevelt).

Are we different Mr. President? Again, are we safer Mr. President? Aren't the images of slaughter still occurring? Or have you asked the mainstream media not to report on them?

32

"We must use terror, assassination, intimidation, land confiscation, and the cutting of all social services to rid Galilee of its Arab population."

The above statement is attributed to David Ben-Gurion, the founding father of the State of Israel and First Israeli Prime Minister taken from Ben-Gurion, a Biography, by Michael Ben-Zohar (May 1948). I am not a historian, but such transgressions aside, it is not too farfetched to suggest that history often repeats itself. Especially when it pertains to presidential politics and nations like Israel, the United States, Syria, Turkey and Iran. Even considering smaller yet significant events ranging from the slaying of Crispus Attucks during the Boston Massacre in 1770 to the signing of the "Southern Manifesto" by Strom Thurman and a hundred plus democratic members of the house, to the operations run by Kermit Roosevelt that caused a coup in Iran in 1959; to even Eisenhower himself and his conundrum regarding Nasser of Egypt inclusive of France, Israel and the Aswan Damn.

This is a week or more after the first presidential debate and I am willing to bet most black folk are still talking about it. Subsequently, given that most are caught up with that circus called the presidential debate, truth be told it is immaterial and all that I mention prior are (albeit) past history more important than the debate when we look at the global predicament and war and our relationship with Israel. You see, although the U.S. has laws that require foreign interests to register as foreign agents, these laws are not equally or always applied to all Israeli lobby groups, such as AIPAC.

Unless you have been behind a rock, you would know that besides the criminal prison and military industrial complexes, the big industry money maker in America is war. Yes, war drives the economy and amounts to more than all of our allocated GDP spent when compared to all other programs in the United States that is if you don't include international aid in the form of grants to nations like Israel, Egypt, Saudi Arabia, Pakistan and Afghanistan. Even as one reads this, Syria is being attacked inside by NATO funded Al Qaeda "Rebels," China and Japan are at each other's throats, shells fly each and every day in the Sudan and Mali is in the middle of a serious conflict.

For a while now, much has been made in political forums of addressing Iran and their quest to become nuclear sufficient (strangely enough by nations who have nuclear weapons - U.S. and Israel). Meaning that regardless of what is being spoken in public, behind closed doors activities show how involved this issue in both political and economic capital.

The U.S., via NATO and the Saudi's are funding dozens of training camps that have been set up to prepare for the fight against President Bashar al-Assad's military. Both U.S. and Saudi millions and special forces expertise are engaged covertly in training Al Qaeda terrorist (FSA Syria's rebels) into a disciplined military force. The FSA or "The Free Syrian Army" didn't exist until Israel, NATO and the U.S. decided that the powers that be needed a war, a major war, to make money and to topple the Syrian leader as well as the state bank of Syria. In fact the same ploy that is being used to break Iran and their independent state bank via the Libyan blue print for the same is being replicated in Syria.

Seems as if those of us in the West, limited by our ignorance and overshadowed by our obsessive ranting on freedom and democracy, cannot comprehend what democracy would mean to a non-Western world dominated by a belief in Islam. We look at what has happened in Libya and what is currently happening in Syria as being singularly about democracy and the development of a secular ideology that includes a pluralistic society run according to democratic principles while those on the ground see it about something completely different - espousing fundamentalism directed exclusive against western aggression and hegemony.

Another issue of concern is confounded when Middle Eastern Nations question the nationalistic approach of the West to their region. For example, the overt hypocrisy of U.S. leadership under President Obama concerned about repression in Syria and Libya but not Bahrain and Saudi Arabia. They wonder how the U.S. continues to evaluate all issues from state perspectives and a monolithic Islam versus Alawite, Sunni and Shī'ah sects of Islam. On the one hand he supposedly is operating a multi-front war, in secrecy against Al Qaeda (Islamic fundamentalism), particularly in Africa and the Middle East – as evident by the increase in size of the U.S. military's Special Forces Operation Command and the CIA's strike expansion capabilities in the region in places including Kenya, Uganda, the Central African Republic, Ethiopia, Djibouti, Mauritania, Burkina Faso and the Seychelles islands in the Indian Ocean off East Africa – while at the same time asserting that they do not desire a conflict with Islam. This albeit our policy pursues wars presently on four fronts: Syria, Lebanon and Iran, and Afghanistan.

We have seen this all before when President Gamal Abdel Nasser's, who had come to power in the 1953 nationalistic revolution in Egypt. Nasser wanted to construct a dam at Aswan, to form a massive lake that would aid to control the annual flooding of the Nile, crucial to Egypt's agriculture, as well as generate vast amounts of electricity. First he was offered economic support by Britain and U.S. to finance the Aswan dam, but then the West backed out.

This led to a buildup of British and French forces in the Mediterranean, with the secret understanding that Israeli troops would move into the Sinai Peninsula. Trying to present a position of peace the European nations asked that both move away from the region and when Egypt disregarded, against the ruling of the UN Security Council and general assembly, Britain and France begin bombing Egyptian airfields. This was under Eisenhower, who although in the open refused to join Britain, France and Israel in an invasion of Egypt, had approved of and knew about such behind closed doors.

Yes the methods of Eisenhower are similar to the methods Obama presently uses, the role of Israel as agent provocateur is the same – making up a threat that doesn't exist because a nation attempts to exist in a self-determined fashion. The only difference is that then it was a damn in Egypt and now it is nuclear power in Iran.

Another common denominator is economics. Then, it pertained to vital shipping routes, today it deals with the Middle East and West Africa as emerging vital oil-producing, mineral rich zones including arable farmland. After the U.S. denied funding Egypt, they went to Russia for military support which was granted. Today, the same is happening in Syria, Iran and also Pakistan. In fact, Pakistani-Russian ties are growing under Russian President Vladimir Putin who is expected to make the first visit by a Russian president to Pakistan ever, supposedly to sign multiple Memorandums of Understanding (MOU'S) on development and investment in the steel and energy sectors of Pakistan. Syria's central role in the Arab gas pipeline is also a key to why Israel, NATO and the U.S. want Assad out, it has a direct path to Iran (just as the Taliban in Afghanistan, they are in the way of the Unocal pipeline).

I guess what I am saying, to repeat myself, is that without war, America's economy would already be in the grave as opposed to on its death bed. War is good economics, no matter if it is in the Middle East, China, the Far East or Africa. The question is will we be able to make money before we realize we may not have the financial ability to carry out such efforts? Right now the United States military has secretly sent a task force of more than 150 specialists to Jordan to be in place in the event that turmoil in Syria expands into a wider conflict.

Unfortunately, it is a fallacy to think or believe that America can be taken out of economic crisis via more and more wars given that the most productive part of the U.S. economy has been moved offshore in order to increase corporate profits and capital gains to equity owners. It is not the American people who are at the center of such policy efforts, like I said; historically it is the war machine and the oligarchy of private interests. More wars that we can only afford to pay with debt spells trouble. It is like having a gallon of gasoline, and pouring a half gallon of water into, it doesn't change the fact of how much gasoline remains. Borrowing more debt, quantitative easing, or printing more loot is the same thing as the above example. It is an invisible tax that just steals tax payer's money through inflation because basic math wins out in the end and shows that the act of printing money doesn't create any more jobs than one already has.

Now, in light of Obama's "neoliberalism, the federal government is just borrowing more loot from itself, loot it doesn't have because the Federal Reserve can print as much as it wants and buy government bonds with the new money it has printed. Such practices are in concert with America's "Ad hoc global 'counter-terrorism' efforts that began under President George W. Bush. The way I think, this means that what can be anticipated in the future is that either the Obama Administration or a Romney Administration will in my estimation, by 2013, have the U.S. at war with Iran just because it is the penchant of Israel, and its nuclear program will be used as a reason for this attack. Although it is well know that Iran doesn't have a nuclear weapon. We already see posturing vis a vis, Turkey, being used as a NATO proxy to get to Syria on a direct path to Iran. As well, there is evidence that the Egypt-Israel peace treaty is slowly evaporating before our eyes. Although we say we desire the impossible dream of secular Islamic or secular Islamic states all across the region that includes a pluralistic society run according to democratic principles, it won't happen now given what has manifested in Syria as I stated earlier.

For decades the Americans indulged and propped up pro-Western dictators in the interests of U.S. foreign policy in the Middle East. Over the last 18 months, four of these dictators have fallen to pro-democracy uprisings, leaving U.S. strategy cold war-esque. And since we're broke and can't make loot via cold war, we will continue to engage in efforts to spark wars around the world, for whatever reason even if they are as petty as what transpired in Egypt and France and Britain – even if we have to adopt the position of David Ben-Gurion, and use terror just to accomplish such.

33

Okay, maybe it is just me, but for some reason I do not see why folk are all up in arms and extremely supportive of Susan Rice. Sometimes I think it is the 98 percent of black folk syndrome that believes Obama or Rice can never be wrong, or make mistakes, intentionally misinform of even worse – never lie.

Rice, I suspect is thought by many to be Obama's top pick for secretary of state, if you asked me, based on what I understand of her statements and her policy, she is dangerously incompetent to be SOS. She is smart, but the only way I can support her selection is if all we want is an incompetent war monger in the office. True, she is a Stanford University graduate and Rhodes Scholar who worked for the reknown McKinsey & Company before she joined the National Security Council under President Bill Clinton, and from there she became President Clinton's assistant secretary of state for African affairs, but job promotion has nothing to do with utility of being a competent SOS.

The merit is there, no question, but when one looks at intent, and attributes siding with liberty, freedom and truth, Rice gets no points. Whether or not she intentionally and willfully misled the American people on the Benghazi attacks, or ran misdirection for the Obama Administration in denying a terror attack prior to his re-election is not the point. The bottom line is that she is not the best choice for the job if you look at the world from the vantage point of an African American who takes prided in having the first African American President albeit I agree with less than 10 percent of his policy – foreign, domestic and economic. Rice is a major point of consternation.

Starting with Africa and Rwanda specifically, Rice's lack of action pertaining to genocide in that nation shows that she has no backbone to assert democracy and liberty on behalf of America. Not to mention the manner in which she should have broken her neck on behalf of the Clinton Administration to deny assistance to the Tutsis. Yes, based on her recommendations as a part of Bill Clinton's National Security Team in 1994, her refusal to suggest action in the Rwandan genocide that left more than 800,000 men, women, and children to be hacked to death by machete in the fastest genocide ever recorded will always be a scarlet letter on her dress and make her this generations Hester Pyrnne.

That was nothing, she even went farther by obstructing the efforts of other nations to stop the slaughter. Instead, although in April 1994 the Canadian UN commandeer in Rwanda, General Romeo Dallaire, declared that he required only 5000 troops to stop the genocide, she advocated that the UN force under Dallaire reduced by ninety percent to 270 troops.

Samantha Power of the Atlantic said it best as the author of the Pulitzer-Prize winning "A Problem of Hell" who referred to Ambassador Susan Rice and her colleagues in the Clinton Administration as Bystanders to Genocide when she quoted Rice in her 2002 book "If we use the word 'genocide' and are seen as doing nothing, what will be the effect on the November congressional election?" Meaning - Rice saw genocide as being less important than partisan politics interests. This is not partisan on Power's behalf, seeing that presently Power currently is a Special Assistant to President Barack Obama.

Rice also has a troubled past as it pertains to the Iraq war and invasion by President Bush which she vehemently supported. In one instance she stated in 2003 to NPR, "I think he has proved that Iraq has these weapons and is hiding them, and I don't think many informed people doubted that." In another, she stated: "It's clear that Iraq poses a major threat. It's clear that its weapons of mass destruction need to be dealt with forcefully, and that's the path we're on. I think the question becomes whether we can keep the diplomatic balls in the air and not drop any, even as we move forward, as we must, on the military side." I can also throw in Libya where she clearly was the main person to move the president to take action against Gaddafi and Syria, where she promoted armed intervention against Syria. In general, Rice has a track record of doing all that I hated George Bush did or attempted to do – advocating nation-building in failed states. Add to this her support for more troops in Afghanistan, she appears to be no different that Rumsfeld or Wolfowitz.

She supports Israel unconditionally, speaking of democracy in Egypt, Libya and Syria but not for Palestinians. And she has not said one word on Israel rounding up Africans to internments and deporting thousands deemed a threat to the

110

Jewish character of the state. She is silent of the rounding up of members of different racial groups and holding them in camps for deportation and the overt hostility towards blacks in general, where the nation or tax payers fund refer to blacks and Africans as a cancer and an AIDs virus on the Israeli people.

Add to the aforementioned incompetency and a policy that seems to support Israel no matter what and African neo-colonialism, she has even more baggage. If she is selected by the President to be SOS, she will have a major conflict of interest. Currently, Rice holds millions of dollars in investments in Canadian oil companies and banks that have keen interest and investments in the $7 billion Keystone XL Pipeline. If she was to become the next Secretary of State, she would have the final say in determining if the pipeline gets approved and built or not. According to the environmental advocacy group Natural Resources Defense Council and financial disclosure reports, Rice has MAJOR INVESTMENTS in more than a dozen Canadian oil companies and banks that would benefit from enhancement of the Canadian tar sands industry and the building of the KPL. Open record reports indicate that approximately a third of Ricc's personal net worth (stimated in 2009 to be between $23.5 million and $43.5 million) is in Canadian oil production and other off shoot markets. Not to mention that Rice has between $300,000 and $600,000 invested in TransCanada, the company trying to get permission from the State Department to construct portions of the KPL from Oklahoma to Canada.

111

When we look at her investments in banks, the conflict of interest issue becomes more lucid. She has "investments totaling at least $5 million and up to $11.25 million in Bank of Montreal, Bank of Nova Scotia, Canadian Imperial Bank of Commerce, Royal Bank of Canada, and Toronto Dominion." A report by the Dutch consulting firm Profundo Economic Research notes that some of these banks are largely responsible for underwriting the expansion of Canada's tar sands industry.

And I will not mention that Rice and her husband own at least $1.25 million worth of stock in four of Canada's eight leading oil producers, as ranked by Forbes magazine including Enbridge, (company responsible for spilling more than a million gallons of toxic bitumen into Michigan's Kalamazoo River in 2010 -- the largest inland oil spill in U.S. history).

Susan Rice is smart, that is not the point, and she just should not be the SOS. Now she may have another stage of genocide on her hands as she did with the invasion of the Democratic Republic of Congo by U.S. allies in Rwanda and Uganda which left six million Congolese dead begining in 1996. Now with the capture of Goma, an eastern Congolese city of one million, by "rebels" under Rwandan and Ugandan control complete with the support of western nations the United States and the United Kingdom (who are arming,training and equipping the Rwandan and Ugandan militaries). After all our U.S. ambassador to the UN Susan Rice is the main one responsible for keeping information on Rwandan and Ugandan role in the ongoing genocide out of international policy. It was Rice who blocked the UN Security Council from demanding that Rwanda endsupport to M23 rebels.

The way I see it anyone who supports Susan Rice either doesn't read, think for themselves or is mentally retarded. The saddest thing about it for me is seeing black folk support her without question. Maybe idiots shouldn't vote

34

Obama and Rice are the only black global leaders to vote against Palestine statehood over the past four years, the Obama Administration in concert with his present U.S. ambassador to the United Nations, Susan Rice, have been speaking of the importance and the need for America and his administration to show world leadership on the importance of democracy to flourish around the globe. Both have spoken vehemently on the importance of supporting democracy in Syria, Libya and Egypt among other nations hit by the Arab protest earlier this year. However, the word democracy is never used by the world's leading black global leaders with respect to Palestine.

Case in point, the overwhelming U.N. vote to elevate the status of Palestine at the world body saw the United States ,via Ambassador Rice on the request of President Obama, vote against the resolution.

Moreover, it showed how the Administration's policy in the Middle East is out of touch with the rest of the globe. Canada, Panama, the Czech Republic and four tiny Pacific island states were the only ones in the 193-member U.N. General Assembly siding with the U.S. against the Palestinian Authority's request for nonmember observer state status in a losing effort resulting in a 138-9 vote, with 41 abstentions in support of the measure. France, Italy, Spain, Norway, Denmark and Turkey were among the U.S. allies voting in support of the resolution. The blatant hypocrisy of this vote on behalf of the United States was made even more political when Ambassador Rice indicated that they were against the motion because it would disrupt the peace process (albeit Obama has not had any success nor made any effort to negotiate a serious peace between Israel and the Palestinians). The issue of Palestinian statehood and self determination has been festering for 65 years regarding mostly territory and sovereignty.

However, it should not be surprising, given the Obama administration sides with Israel as U.S. foreign policy in the region has done historically, making no real effort t support a two state solution. Not to mention the Israeli government can do what it pleases to violate civil rights and the Obama Administration will look away. To date the Obama Administration and Ambassador Rice have yet to speak against Israel's treatment of African Immigrants and refugees – burning and closing their stores, rounding them up like Apartied South Africa and holding them in detention centers as Hilter once did the Jews.

Speaking of Africans, Prime Minister Benjamin Netanyahu suggest that African immigrants threaten the Jewish character of Israel and that all Blacks will on arrival be placed

114

immediately in the many detention centers and containment camps to house tens of thousands. One opinion poll showed 52 percent of Israelis agree that the Africans are "a cancer".

Obama and Rice will never speak out against Israel although not doing so shows their selective views on democracy, especially as the only two major world leaders not to side by Palestinian statehood and self-determination. In many respects it's as if they support apartied over the rights and liberties of the people.

35

When I think of Mali, or any part of West Africa, I often say to myself, I had a ball when I was there in 1992 and 1993. At the time I was living in Owerri, in Southeastern Nigeria. If you have ever seen the Sahel, what typically sticks out from a geopolitical locution is that it runs from the Atlantic Ocean to the Red Sea.

The country, inclusive of the history of the Dogon and those who inhabit the Mopti river region of that great historic place, may be the location of America's next war of western imperialism and neocolonial fervor. To top it all off, it will be carried out via the instruction of the first African America president in the history of the United States.

It seems that Obama's drone wars will have to find a new country to target since the U.S. will be ending its occupation of Afghanistan soon. And since the Administration's war on terror has not ended, the obvious next place to send U.S.

and UN troops is Africa, specifically Mali. I know we have U.S. troops in the Congo, Uganda, Somalia and several other nations, but I have an inclination that Obama will be in this West African nation soon.

All of this would have been unnecessary if the administration had not taken the actions via the UN it did in Libya. In fact, Mali was a stable democracy for the last few decades until we destabilized it. Not only did it lead to arms from Libya flooding the northern region of the nation, it also led to the influx of al-Qaeda affiliated Islamists in the North.

Some would say that I am making this entire thing up. However, I would say that they have not been reading or paying attention or worse, they do not evaluate historical actions that would suggest that the Obama Administration would be supportive of Western military forces in Mali. The U.S. in concert with the UN has conducted armed interventions (with support from Obama). We saw such in Libya where via the UN, Obama, although in direct violation of the U.S. constitution, never consulted congress to overthrow the leader of a sovereign nation even though it required supporting militarily, Islamic fundamentalist militants and Al Qaeda and resulted in the ethnic cleansing and lynching of thousands black Africans.

We also saw such when the Obama Administration and the UN aided in the violent overthrow of the president of the Ivory Coast although the nation's highest court said that he had won the election. He was subsequently replaced by a UN hand-picked Muslim central banker. This too resulted in the death of thousands most of which were Christians.

We are already hearing the administration and UN drop little hints about al Qaeda having set up in northern Mali, right next to Boko Haram in Nigeria. Not to mention the Islamic Maghreb, al Shabab in East Africa. The story is being laid out by Robert Fowler of the UN. In addition, last year the UN Security Council unanimously adopted a resolution "determining that the situation in Mali constitutes a threat to international peace and security." The resolution also noted that the UN was ready to deploy an "international military force" to invade the country if such is seemed necessary.

Stranger is the fact that this is all coming from the urging of the Obama State Department, that the idea of invading Mali is to prop up the interim government. The Obama administration has also been increasing military aid to leaders of ruling countries around Mali in preparation for the upcoming intervention. Not to mention that last year, President Obama ended all of Mali's trade privileges with the U.S., citing backtracking from democracy in the annual assessment of benefits conferred by the Africa Growth and Opportunity Act (AGOA) program. Funny, the way I see it, taking the limited benefits they had under the prior arrangements will only push prospects for democracy farther away, especially given that he approved such with the South Sudan, who is in conflict with Sudan. Mali only exported about $7 million from precious stones, gold, art and antiques, while imports from the U.S. exceeded $40 million. But that's right; the South Sudan has the plentiful Abyei oil region.

Funny, Mali used to be Africa's democratic success stories, now it may be the next Somalia, or even worse – Afghanistan. If the president does involve U.S. military forces in Mali, it will be a tacit confession that his actions in Libya failed and really served to undermine international peace and security. It will reveal to history that his Libyan interventionist policy was his biggest foreign policy mistake and that helping Africa is the farthest thing from his policy perspectives when compared to the old imperialistic agenda of raping the continent of all its natural resources while killing millions via war, starvation, poverty and drought in the process. Yes, Mali may be Obama's Afghanistan and all because there is gold in them there hills. After all, Mali is Africa's third largest gold producer after South Africa and Ghana. Mali produced 537 tons of gold in 2009.

36

It seems like if you're a Western powerhouse nation with economic problems out the wazoo, the retro chic thing to do is not to go to the Grammy's but rather head to Africa. Truth be told, while the west has been buried in the economic doldrums of inflation and recession, Africa has proffered to be home of some of the world's riskiest yet most profitable markets. The MSCI index has grew more than 8 percent in 2012 and is outpacing all the developed stock markets in Japan, the U.S. and

Europe. And you can best believe that both the Federal Reserve and European Central Bank are taking note.

Now true, under President Barack Obama's economic policies the U.S. companies have enjoyed massive profits and corporations' after-tax profits have leaped 171% (more than under any president since World War II). But the reality remains that the American economy, unless you're are a rich corporation or campaign donor who's on the top and has a real shot at getting some of that stimulus loot, you aint hitting on shit. With limited resources and a declining value of the dollar, we're doing what the Romans and King Leopold did – subsidizing and pillaging countries with resources of value. Just so happens we have picked regions of Western and Central Africa.

Now true, on the surface poli-tricksters and main stream media will say our interest in Africa has everything to do with democracy and supporting the people and their interest. However, the facts could be no farther away, and the truth even farther. From the West's purview, the grassroots concerns of the folk don't matter to us. All we want to do is do what we do best - intervene to protect interest we speculate we have in the region as interventionists.

Let us start with the sweet crude oil producing state of Nigeria. I know Nigeria well. I lived there for more than a year in the early 1990s. Nigeria's natural resources include but are not limited to petroleum (sweet crude oil), tin, columbite, iron ore, coal, limestone, lead, zinc, and natural gas. Mali, like

Nigeria, is rich with bauxite, copper, diamonds, gold, granite, gypsum, iron ore, kaolin, limestone, lithium, manganese, phosphates, salt, silver, uranium, and zinc.. Add to the mix Libya, where we know Gaddafi is dead, killed right when he was trying to instigate a United States of Africa to rival all western nations, they have oil and the Bouri Field, the biggest platform in the Mediterranean Sea, not to mention the non-oil manufacturing and construction sectors, as well as iron, steel and aluminum. We must not forget the Congo with their iron ore, magnesium, diamonds, potash, phosphate, copper, lead, zinc, gold and more recently oil.

Uganda has large quantities of natural resources also including gold, diamonds, iron ore, nickel, cobalt, tantalum, niobium, other rare earth elements, and OIL. The government there is in battle with the U.S. and large multi-national oil conglomerates as we speak because they don't want, and rightly so, any foreign oil firms running their shit. Uganda's Lake Albert region is rich with oil.

Although Somalia produces small quantities of uranium, their biggest asset is their location – right up the street and around the corner from the strait of Hormiz and Iran.

Knowing that the aforementioned nations are rich, it places our actions and those of other western European nations into a more lucid perspective. US/NATO operations in Libya in 2011 are an example of that. This means that our actions and interest in Africa are guided by a single basic, imperial and neocolonialist principle. Simply put, as the legendary rapper Biz Markie sang, "you, you got what I want, you got what I need", all under the guidance (supposedly) of Obama's presidential policy directive on Sub-Saharan Africa. I would go into detail on that but I know many black folk don't read and wouldn't know what the newspeak of promoting opportunity and development; spurring economic growth, trade and investment; advancing peace and security; and to strengthen democratic institutions means in main street people terms – RAPE.

The reason America and other European nations are in Africa is geoeconopolitical (yes, I made the word up). The goal is 'creative destruction' in an effort to replace the old African order with a Western-dominated , puppet state, that will serve the national and corporate interest of the nation's doing the dirty work and the banking interests they represent. The way the big Wall St and global bankers see it, Africa is the continent that can make them loot the good-ole boy, neocolonial imperialistic exploitation way. And we can see that with all the U.S. military Obama has placed all over the continent via AFRICOM.

The mission of AFRICOM is to protect the national interests of the United States. And although they are only capable of military action, what they can do is misdirect and destabilize and we all know investment bankers make most of their loot via destabilization. Yes, if the West wants to get loot, they will make up any excuse to do so even if it is an emotion called terror. But yawl don't hear me though, especially black folk who feel as if the black half of Obama is running the

Whitehouse and that he actually cares about black folk as much and equally as he does Wall Street. The black folk who don't read and think he walks on water won't care and will likely be my most vocal critics. Yes, Mali don't won't no crackers, even half white, half black ones living in a white house.

37

Around the globe, in particular in African and Asian (Middle Eastern) nations, the typical U.S. policy has been and continues to be the Bushian agenda of destabilizing and genocide. I describe it as Bushian because although such is historical U.S. policy in general, when we cannot buy of an autocratic dictator or start a war, in the modern era it began with Bush 41, specifically when President George H. Bush sent 28,000 U.S. troops to Somalia to do what he described as "God's work." Although he promised the American people that our military would "not stay one day longer than is absolutely necessary," we ended up being there for almost two years before President Bill Clinton suddenly ended the mission in 1993.

The price of the UN/U.S. mission was heavy: 24 Pakistani UN peacekeepers inspecting a weapons site were ambushed and killed by Somalia soldiers under the warlord General Mohammed Aidid, 18 Elite Delta Force soldiers were killed and 84 wounded during an assault on Mogadishu's Olympia Hotel in search of Aidid. Although it was said the mission was to help deliver food aid, it became visibly clear the goal was to remove General Mohammed Aidid from power.

122

As well as be in the position to control oil and gas reserves, since Aidid would block the permission granted to several large multi-national oil corporations from the Somalia president Siad Barre to search for oil. Not forgetting that Somalia has the largest coastline in Africa, part of which. One part of this coastline is just in front of the most important region in the world for the moment, the Middle East. Another part of the coastline faces the Indian Ocean.

From my narrow-mindedness, it appears that the goal of President Obama currently has nothing to do with growing democracy and protecting the citizens of Syria, but more so with the removal of President Bashar Assad. And as in Somalia, natural resources reinforce or interventionist agenda, especially considering the news that Iraq has approved the construction of a 900 plus mile natural gas pipeline that will connect Iran to Syria. I am almost certain this plays into the rationale for taking down President Bashar Assad as well.

In East Africa today, there are still Somalis living in the neighboring countries of Ethiopia, Kenya, and Djibouti. Likewise, it was just reported that more than a million Syrians are now refuges in the neighboring nations of Lebanon, Jordan, Turkey and Iraq due to the two years of U.S. instigating violence across Syria.

Since our intervention in Somalia, what has happened? One, the Tigray People's Liberation Front (TPLF) regime of Zenawi Meles in Ethiopia has sent its troops into Somalia and their main goal was to create the independent Republic of Tigray. Then the EPLF (Eritrean People Liberation Front) from Eritrea that was occupied by Ethiopia, stepped in the political and military picture. Then in 2006, a group of high-ranking officers led by General Kamal Galchuu joined the Oromo Liberation Front. In the Orome area a real intifada started up and a few months ago, the OLF launched an appeal to all opposition groups to join the united front ADF (Alliance for Democracy and Freedom). All of this eventually led to incessant social and political destabilization and, you guessed it, a nation stabilized via Islamic fundamentalist and anti-US rule via Islamist who did what America couldn't (defeat the warlords and liberate the entire nation whole country in six months).

What we saw in Somalia, was the result of U.S. government meddling. All fueled by the United States' support of unpopular warlords, who once the Somalia people found out they were being supported by the U.S., made the popularity of the Islamist movement more appealing. Plus the manner in which the U.S. backed Ethiopia and their indiscriminate shelling of Mogadishu's civilian areas didn't make it easier for anything other than a stronger hatred of America.

Now we see the same thing again. President Obama has stated that Assad has lost his legitimacy as a leader. In Mexico his position was outlined more specifically when while in Los Cabos, Mexico, he pointed fingers at Russia and China saying that they have "not signed on" to any plan that promotes the removal of Bashar al-Assad's from power.

Truth be told the Obama administration doesn't want a solution for they don't believe there is any solution that exist that would curb the violence that leaves him in power. The reason there is no diplomatic solution to the conflict in Syria is because the Obama Administration doesn't desire one. They want to continue to implement a policy of Bushian destabilization in Syria, they want Assad to go or be killed instead of what the Syrian People want.

The Obama Administration is trying with its all it has to make a case for more support for al- Qaeda rebels he calls the FSA and sequentially describing their actions as leading a popular uprising against an "illegitimate" government.

Assad on the other hand is saying that it is at war with "terrorists." If history is any indication, we will end up with a divided Syria that will eventually become a series of small states like and at best, and at worse, a nation run by rise of warlords and militias; just as we saw in Somalia. Just like Iraq and Afghanistan - even if folk do not want such or even if we fail. But when other folks use our idealistic tendencies it becomes sacrilegious.

Our "imperial arrogance" asserts I guess, that the only folks with rights to a free and pen society on us and no one else. We have the audacity to proclaim being open, democratic and proponents of the free sharing of information unless it pertains to information of ours. Then we become the incarnate of Mussolini and fascism. The expression is obviously OK except for the Internet. Why? I cannot answer, but I can say we use our power to make private enterprises including PayPal and Amazon.com and master card to control what the supreme courts have considered expression as well - money when anything we disagree with is cited or revealed. It is just ridiculous, the greatest democracy in the world asking for an Internet site to be shut down and its owner killed or jailed for sharing information that he did not steal.

How quick we are to reference Thomas Jefferson but forget it was he who wrote, "Information is the currency of democracy." I just find it two-faced to say on the one hand we are a Nation of liberty and freedom yet on the other hold freedom of the Internet as being completely different. Even condemning China for their censorship but we espouse the same behavior and practice from a governmental location regarding Wikileaks. Common sense tells me that if one condemns WikiLeaks we have to do the same with the New York Times and other websites.

Freedom in the US is a myth. This is the only postulate that can be contrived from this entire WikiLeaks fiasco. Such is even more convoluted when we have no laws to even assert criminal behavior on the websites owners behalf outside of an outdated 1917 espionage act that deals with maps.

ABOUT THE AUTHOR

Torrance Stephens is originally from Memphis, Tennessee. He attended Morehouse College where he studied, psychology, biology and chemistry. He received a master's degree in Educational Psychology and Measurement from Atlanta University and a Ph.D. in Counseling from Clark Atlanta University. He has lived in Nigeria, Senegal, South Africa and several other African countries working with Africare International and conducting Infectious disease research. He is the author of several books including a novel, poems, essays and several collections of short prose. He was an Assistant Professor at Emory University in the Rollins School of Public Health in Atlanta for more than 14 years and until recently, as Associate Professor and Health Education/Health Promotion Track Coordinator for the MPH program at Morehouse School of Medicine in the Department of Community and Preventive Medicine. He is the father of two and currently lives in Palmetto, Georgia, and teaches Statistics at Clark Atlanta University in the Departments of Psychology and School of Education.

www.ingramcontent.com/pod-product-compliance
Lightning Source LLC
Chambersburg PA
CBHW072139280526
45788CB00002B/710